Finding Peace, Joy, and Unity

A Bible Study on the Book of Philippians

A.J. Paris

ISBN 978-1-64003-214-9 (Paperback)
ISBN 978-1-64003-215-6 (Digital)

Scripture taken from the NEW AMERICAN STANDARD BIBLE®, Copyright © 1960,1962,1963,1968,1971,1972,1973,1975,1977,1995 by The Lockman Foundation. Used by permission

Scripture quotations marked (NIV) are from The Holy Bible, New International Version®. NIV®. Copyright © 1973,1978, 1984 by Biblia. Used by permission of Zondervan. All rights reserved. www.zondervan.com.

Covenant Books, Inc.
11661 Hwy 707
Murrells Inlet, SC 29576
www.covenantbooks.com

Week One, Day One: Why Study the Bible?

Before we jump into studying the book of Philippians, we first need to realize why we are studying it. This might seem odd to you, but I hope you will bear with me through today's study. Hopefully, at the end, you will see why it is important to ask this question.

I love going to Bible study! I have a group of women from my church who love to meet together and study the Word of God. It is always a great time to share what God is doing in our lives. Recently, my pastor preached a sermon that really hit me hard. He made the comment that Christians should not just sit around and study the Bible together without applying what they have learned to their everyday lives. I think that my Bible study group has been trying to apply what we have learned to our lives and to our church, but we could all strive to do more.

Therefore, I want to try and help you learn God's Word well, and then apply His book to your life. First, why do you study the Bible?

Why do you want to do this particular Bible study?

I am sure most of you wrote down things like "to grow closer to God," or "to learn how God wants me to live my life," and some of you might have said, "I love the book of Philippians." All of these are great answers, but there are some wrong reasons to study the Bible. The top two wrong reasons for studying the Bible are guilt and status.

When we study the Bible because of guilt, we think that we *have* to read our Bibles every day or God will get mad at us. We put a certain time limit on how long we must spend studying our Bible so we can feel that God will be pleased with us. We need to realize that God wants us to study His Word and pray, so we can have a closer relationship with Him. Yes, He wants to spend quality time with you as much as possible, but it is not about filling in a certain time limit to please Him. If you miss a day of Bible reading, tell God you are sorry and your guilt should go away because you are forgiven. If you forget to call your best friend one day, would they stop being your friend? No, you would just say you are sorry and then pick back up and see what you missed that day. So, please, do not study the Bible so you do not feel guilty. You wouldn't want your best friend spending time with you out of guilt, so don't treat God like that!

Next is status. Sometimes Christians study the Bible so they can look good in front of other Christians. They want to brag and say that they have read the whole Bible. Or brag and say that they meet once a week with a group of friends to study the Bible. They tell their friends (who are not a part of their Bible study) this, and try to make them feel bad because their friends do not go to a weekly Bible study. We should never study the Bible just so we can look better in front of others. We need to check our motivation.

Do you struggle with either of these wrong reasons for studying the Bible? If so, write about it below.

We also need to realize that the Bible is God's Word to us. When we open the Bible and study it, God is right beside and speaking to us. There are so many good reasons for studying the Bible. I have a long list below. Please check all of the good reasons for studying the Bible.

o   So we can learn more about God
o   So we can learn more about the world we live in
o   So we can live the godly lives He wants us to live
o   So we can have a right relationship with God
o   So we can learn more about Jesus
o   So we can be prepared to go on mission for God
o   So we can better understand the mind of God
o   So we can learn to praise God
o   _____ (other reasons you might want to add)
o   _____

After reading this list, doesn't it make you excited about reading and studying God's Word? The author of Psalm 119 loved God's Word! He loved it so much that he wrote the longest psalm in the Bible, and it is *all* about God's Word! Let's look at a few verses from Psalm 119.

Write out a summary of each verse:

Psalm 119:1–2 _____

Psalm 119:11 _____

Psalm 119:105 _____

Psalm 119:110 _____

Psalm 119:127 _____

Psalm 119:131 _____

Psalm 119:161 _____

Pick the verse that means the most to you and explain why.

We should love the Word of God as much as the author who wrote Psalm 119. We should love it so much that we don't just read it, but we study and try to apply it in as many ways in our lives as we possibly can. No area of our lives should be left unattended when it comes to applying God's Word.

Read Hebrews 4:12. What does this verse say about the Word of God?

According to James 1:22–25, what should we not do? What should we do?

Now, read Jesus's words in Luke 11:28, what did Jesus say in this verse?

I am sure most of you have heard of Pinterest. Many of you might use Pinterest on a regular basis. Many people love to spend hours on Pinterest planning parties or searching for recipes, or maybe looking up fun crafts. Pinterest is a great way to look up all kinds of things! But a lot of times, people *pin* things onto Pinterest but they never really do these things. If you go to their Pinterest and look at what they have pinned, you might be very impressed but you have no way of knowing if they really have done any of those things. We must stop being Pinterest Christians! Pinterest Christians go to church and look good on the outside. They could even go to Bible study but never take what they learn and apply it to their lives. It is as if they have pinned it but never do it. Pinterest Christians may think "It's okay, I have all the information about how to live my life, and I can just pull it out when I need it." We don't need to study the Bible just for knowledge that we can use at some other time in our lives. We need to apply it now! We need to study the Bible, apply, and obey it right now. We will miss out on God's blessings when we don't do this.

I love what Francis Chan said in his book *Multiply* about studying the Bible.

> "Though we primarily think of the Bible as something we read in order to gain knowledge, we actually have it backward. The Bible reads us- it penetrates to our core and expresses who we really are. If you ever find yourself reading your Bible and not changing, then you can

be sure that you're approaching the Bible in the wrong way. It's not about finding support for our lifestyle or way of thinking; it's about approaching the mind of God and letting Him change and redefine who we are."

Are you willing and ready for God's Word to change you?

I am going to ask you to do three things to help you make sure you know how to apply what you learn from this Bible study. First, I want you to pray each time you sit down to read this Bible study. Pray that God will open your heart so He can speak to you. Pray while you are reading this study that God will help you to understand that day's scripture. Pray that God will show you how to apply these truths to your own life, and pray that God will give you the power to apply these truths.

Read Psalm 119:15, 23, 27, and 97. What is the one word that was in each verse?

Second, I want for you to meditate on God's Word. Many Christians might think that meditation is something bad, but meditating on God's Word is not bad, it's biblical! When you meditate on God's Word, you're reflecting on it during your day. You ask God how you should apply it. Instead of worrying, you think about a passage of scripture. Instead of daydreaming, you ponder the meaning to a Bible verse. When you meditate on God's Word, you try to wrap your brain around the meaning and application of a Bible verse or a passage every moment you are free to think. I think if we spend more time immersing our thoughts in God's words, we will grow like never before. At the beginning of each week, you will pick your Bible verses to meditate on for the rest of the week. You just need to pick one verse per week.

Each day, I want for you to begin your day in prayer, and I will also give you extra space to write down your thoughts about your Bible verse. I want you to use this space to analyze the Bible verse you picked. My brain is an overanalytical brain, so I like to break apart scriptures. I want you to think of your verse as a love note that God passed to you in school. Over analyze it like you would have any love note you got when you were young.

I remember when my husband and I were *talking* and had not admitted to each other that we liked each other yet. He said something to me, and I then overanalyzed it and thought that he did not like me. I then went online and posted a very odd comment online, and he analyzed my comment and realized that I was confused. Soon after that, he called me and asked me out for our first date. That is just a little fun story to show that we analyze situations *all* the time!

When you analyze your scripture, I want for you to look for several things.

Here is a list:

Words that are repeated (this also includes phrases)
Contrasting statements (these focus on differences, make sure you note who or what is being contrasted)
Statements that compare things (look for things or people that have similarities)
Any kind of list
Cause and effect statements (hint: look for the words *if* and *then*. There could also be more than one effect, so look out for those)

Figures of speech (look for phrases where the words should not be taken literally)

Conjunctions (look for words like *and, but,* and *for.* Make sure you also note what the conjunctions are connecting)

Verbs (look for action verbs where the subject is the one doing the action. Also note the tense of the verb)

Pronouns (make sure you note the antecedent for all the pronouns)

Emotional language (look for words like *love* and other words that express emotions)

As you use the space I provided daily to analyze your Bible verse, look back at the above list. Look for each thing in your Bible verse. Then, write down what you notice. I personally like to circle, box off, number lists, and draw around the Bible verses. It helps me. It is up to you if you want to do this or not.

I have one more thing I am going to ask you to do each week. The third is I want for you to memorize the Bible verse that you pick. (These verses will be called our M and M verses because we will meditate on them and memorize them) You might say that you can't memorize. Do you know your address? Do you know your phone number? Do you know John 3:16? If you answered yes to any of those questions, then yes you can memorize! Don't feel guilty if you don't get it done. Remember, we do not study the Bible out of guilt! I think that when you meditate on this verse, it will be easier for you to memorize it.

Ralph Moore said in his book *Making Disciples* that "obedience requires action, but action always starts with a simple decision to do whatever God ask of us." Are you ready to obey God? Are you willing to say right now before we even start studying the book of

Philippians that you are going to obey God and put into action what He shows you?

If you are ready to be changed by the Word of God, then I ask that you sign your name below as a commitment in front of God that you will study the book of Philippians, and use God's power in you to be able to apply His teachings to your everyday life.

Signature: _____

Date: _____

I hope you are excited about this study. I know I am!

Week One M and M Bible Verses

Please pick one Bible verse to meditate on this week, and memorize it. Feel free to write it on a note card so you can carry it around with you, or try to think of other fun ways that you can keep the Bible verse close by! I am using NIV on this page so you can easily look at them and pick the one you want to use, but please use the translation you like the most.

"About midnight Paul and Silas were praying and singing hymns to God, and the other prisoners were listening to them" (Acts 16:25).

"At once he began to preach in the synagogues that Jesus is the Son of God" (Acts 9:20).

"I have hidden your word in my heart that I might not sin against you" (Psalms 119:11).

"Cause me to understand the way of your precepts that I may meditate on your wonderful deeds" (Psalm 119:27).

Week One, Day Two: Saul's Conversion

Start today with prayer. Pray that God will open your heart, speak to you, help you understand this scripture, show you how to apply these truths, and give you the power to apply His Word to your life.

On the space below, write out your Bible verse for this week. Then, spend at least five minutes analyzing the scripture. Refer to day one so you can remember what you need to be looking for.

_____
_____
_____
_____
_____
_____
_____
_____
_____
_____
_____
_____
_____
_____

Today, we are going to be learning about the Apostle Paul. Growing up, I always viewed Paul as the enemy of the early church. Yes, he did persecute the early church, but he did this because he thought he was following the right god! I should also note that at this time, Paul was called Saul. Most Christians believe that God changed Saul's name to Paul, but if you study Acts 13:9, you will notice that it just says that Saul started going by the name Paul. Saul was his Hebrew name. Paul was the Roman version of his name. It is believed that once Saul was called by God to preach to the Gentiles that Saul started going by Paul because the Gentiles would have been more familiar with the name Paul. But for today's lesson, to try to make things easy for you to understand, I will call him Saul if I am talking about something that happened before Acts 13:9, and I will call him Paul if it is something that happened after Acts 13:9.

Saul grew up in a Jewish family and even went to Jerusalem for training to become a rabbi. He would have known the Old Testament very well. After Jesus's death and resurrection, many Jews were realizing that Jesus was the Messiah they had been waiting for, but Saul did not believe in Jesus. He thought that these people who were following Jesus were being led astray by a false teacher.

Read Deut. 21:23. According to this verse, who is cursed by God?

Saul knew this verse, and most likely did not think that Jesus could be the Messiah if he was cursed by God. Luckily, after Saul's conversation, he saw the cross in a different light.

Read what Paul wrote in Galatians 3:13–14. Why did Jesus become a curse for us?

Read Deut. 13:1–5.

What were they to do if someone started telling them to follow someone other than the Lord their God?

Why were they told to do this?

Saul would have known this scripture as well, which brings us to the first Christian killed for following Jesus in the Bible.

Read Acts 6:8–14. What was Stephen doing?

Did the Jews agree with him? How did they handle the situation?

People had already accused Stephen of trying to lead them away from the Lord. Then, Stephen gives a long speech and goes through a summary of the whole Old Testament. We are going to pick up at the end of his speech. Read Acts 7:51–60.

What did Stephen call them?

What did they do to Stephen?

Who was holding the coats?

I am sure that the Jews did not like being called *stiff-necked* and people with *uncircumcised hearts*. I think both the accusations made about Stephen and his words toward the Jews made the Jews think they were justified with stoning him to death. I think these Jews did not realize that God was not happy with their actions. They really thought that God would be pleased with them.

Now read Acts 8:1–4. How did Saul feel about the Jews stoning Stephen?

What did Saul then do?

What happened to the Christians? Did they stop telling others about Jesus?

The Christians did not let this persecution stop them from spreading the good news of the Gospel. They were willing to tell others about Jesus even if they were beaten, imprisoned, or killed. God used their boldness to spread the Gospel in a great way. Persecution is another topic that we are going to be talking about during this Bible study.

Now read Acts 9:1–21.

What was Saul doing while he waited to regain his sight? (verse 11)

I had never noticed this before. Saul was most likely scared and did not realize what all that was going on, so he prayed. God had to get Saul's attention, and He did it in a big way. Saul turned to prayer because if Jesus really was who He said He was, God would hear Saul's prayer and send him help.

What was Ananias called? Why did Ananias not want to go to Saul? (verse 10)

Fill in the blank (I am using the New American Standard Version):

"So, Ananias departed and entered the house, and after laying his hands on him said, 'Brother Saul, the Lord Jesus, who appeared to you on the road by which you were coming, has sent me so that you may regain your sight and be filled with the Holy Spirit.' And _____ there fell from his eyes something like scales, and he regained his sight, and he got up and was baptized. Now for several days he was with the disciples who were at Damascus, and _____ he began to proclaim Jesus in the synagogues, saying, and 'He is the Son of God'" (Acts 9:17–20).

God used Ananias to immediately heal Saul. Saul then turned around and started telling others about Jesus.

Write down some of the things Jesus has done for you. (Yes, list *dying for your sins*, but also list other things as well) Do you think about these things often?

Saul saw God work immediately in his own life and could not wait to tell others. I pray for all of the people doing this study (and for myself) that God will help us to see and understand all that He has done for us. From Jesus's life, death, resurrection, and all the ways He has worked in our lives since. When we see how God has helped us, we will naturally want to turn around and immediately tell others about Him! This was just the start of Paul telling others about Jesus.

Week One, Day Three:
Background on Philippians

Start today with prayer. Pray that God will open your heart, speak to you, help you understand this scripture, show you how to apply these truths, and give you the power to apply His Word to your life.

On the space below, write out your Bible verse for this week. Then, spend at least five minutes analyzing the scripture. Refer to day one so you can remember what you need to be looking for.

_____

_____

_____

_____

_____

_____

_____

_____

_____

_____

_____

_____

Today, we are going to be reading in the Book of Acts where Paul is called to go to Philippi, and what happens while he is there.

Read Acts 16:6–10.

Name the places where Paul and Silas tried to go but the Holy Spirit stopped them.

What did the person say in the vision?

When I first read this scripture, I thought about how God closed doors on Paul and told him not go to certain places, but then God opened the door to where he wanted him to go. I wanted to connect this in our lives when God closes doors to certain things. I was reading this scripture thinking about God taking something away from Paul, but that was not the case! We need to understand that Paul was seeking to serve God. Paul was on a journey to tell others about Christ. He was not just sitting in a house waiting to hear from God. Paul was on his way to Asia when God stopped him. Then, Paul started going toward Mysia but Paul was stopped again. Then, Paul went to Troas and it was there that God told Paul where to go next. When God closed a door on Paul, he was okay with it because he wanted to serve God so much that he just kept seeking and asking God until Paul figured out where God wanted him to go next. I don't think Paul saw this situation as God closing a door to a certain ministry. I think Paul just kept moving forward and waited on God to see exactly where He wanted him to serve next.

Has God ever told you not to be involved with one ministry because He had different plans? If so, write about the situation below.

Do you seek God and how He wants to use you to help spread His Gospel? If so, what has God told you? If not, ask Him now where He wants for you to help spread the Gospel and write down what He tells you (you might have to pray more than once on this one).

Do you trust that God will show you where He wants you to serve?

We should all be involved in sharing the Gospel with the people around us.

What can you do personally in your own life to make sure you are growing closer to Christ and sharing Jesus with others?

Read Acts 16:11–15.

How soon did Paul leave for Macedonia? (*Note the version below*)

"After he had seen the vision, we immediately made efforts to set out for Macedonia, concluding that God had called us to evangelize them" (Acts 16:10 NASB).

Do you immediately follow God when He tells you to do something? If not, what gets in your way?

Philippi was not like the other cities where Paul preached and ministered before. Normally, Paul would go to cities where there was a large synagogue and preach there first. Philippi did not have any synagogues. It did have the main highway from Asia to the west, so this might have been why Paul went to this city first.

According to verse 12, what is another reason why Paul might have picked Philippi?

Since there was not a synagogue, Paul went to the river or *place of prayer* to talk to the people. While there, Paul meets Lydia and she is converted.

What do we know about Lydia from this passage?

Many things stick out to me about Lydia, and I feel that I could do a whole day's Bible study just on her. But since this is a background day for the book of Philippians, I am going to refrain and just note a key thing about this section of the passage.

Who opened Lydia's heart?

God was already working in Philippi before Paul even got there. How wonderful is it to realize that God is working in so many places and so many lives, but He invites us to be involved in sharing the

Gospel with them? It is important to note that God opened her heart, not Paul. Paul was just obeying God and was in the right place.

If God is working on people's hearts to get them ready to hear the Gospel, then why are we so scared to share the Gospel?

Does it make you less scared to know that God is already preparing the hearts of people around you so you can share the Gospel with them?

Stop right now, pray, and ask God to show you whose heart He is preparing so you can share the Gospel with them. Write down any names God gives you below.

What did Lydia offer to Paul?

Since Lydia sold purple cloth, she would have had a lot of money, and therefore, had a big enough house for Paul and his friends to stay in and start their ministry. Is it a coincidence that the first person who was converted in Philippi just happened to open their home to Paul? I think not. God was working. Not only was God already working to get the people of Philippi ready to hear the message of the Gospel, but He was already taking care of Paul and his friends.

How can you see God working in your life to help get you ready to share the Gospel with the people around you?

If you can't see God working in your life, pray and ask Him to reveal how He is working. Close today by praying and asking God where He is working in your life to prepare you to serve Him in sharing the Gospel.

Week One, Day Four: Background to Philippians

Start today with prayer. Pray that God will open your heart, speak to you, help you understand this scripture, show you how to apply these truths, and give you the power to apply His Word to your life.

On the space below, write out your Bible verse for this week. Then, spend at least five minutes analyzing the scripture. Refer to day one so you can remember what you need to be looking for.

_____

_____

_____

_____

_____

_____

_____

_____

_____

_____

_____

_____

_____

Read Acts 16:16–24.

What did the slave girl say about Paul?

I'm not sure why it took Paul hearing this girl several days before he commanded the spirit to come out of her (maybe he knew it would cause trouble), but it happened and a whole lot of trouble happened because of it.

What did the owners accuse Paul of in front of the magistrates? (Verses 20–21)

This was not a true accusation, but the owners knew that they could cause trouble by saying this. Rome had two classifications for religion—legal, and illegal. The rulers in Philippi would have seen Christianity as a sect of Judaism which was a legal religion. Later, they would have realized that Christianity was different from Judaism (although, really, Christianity is the fulfillment of Judaism), *but* since this is the first time that Paul is preaching to these people, they would not have understood.

Who joined in on the attack? (Verse 22)

What did the chief magistrates do to them in front of the mob?

What order was given to the jailer and how did he carry out those orders?

The owners of the slave girl falsely accused Paul and Silas. The magistrates should have listened to Paul and Silas. There should have been a hearing or trial of some kind. Since there was a mob of angry people, the magistrates did not follow the law, and instead, had Paul and Silas beaten to appease the mob.

Can you think of another time in the scripture when someone was falsely accused and beaten because of an angry mob? (Hint: Read Mark 15:6–15)

Have you ever been treated unfairly because you are a Christian? If so, write about it below.

Paul and Silas were stripped of their clothes, beaten, and imprisoned. The jailer was told to make sure they were in the most secure part of the jail.

Try to put yourself in their shoes. Imagine you were stripped of your clothes (yeah, what woman wants that to happen to them in public? I think I would rather just get beaten harder than to have my clothes taken away), beaten, and put into the most secure part of a jail literally in chains. How would you have felt? How would you have reacted if you had been in this situation with Paul and Silas?

Now read Acts 16:25.

What were Paul and Silas doing? What time was it?

Read Matthew 5:11–12 (remember, Jesus is speaking here) and summarize below.

Why do you think Paul and Silas were singing praises to God and praying?

I think that they were happy to be persecuted for God. I think they had been praising God for a long time since it was around midnight. That is hard to wrap our minds around. Here in America, we do not welcome persecution. I think we should strive to be in situations where we have to rely on God. I think that when we are persecuted, we grow stronger to God. We will talk more about persecution when we get to the book of Philippians (and I am so excited about it).

Now, let's read the rest of the story. Read Acts 16:26–38.

So not only have Paul and Silas been beaten, but now here comes a *violent earthquake*. Earthquakes were common in this area, so this would not have been a surprise to the people who lived there. But God brought this earthquake at just the right time. Put yourself back in Paul and Silas's place. If I had been with them and was mature enough to be singing praises and praying to God, when that earthquake hit, I think I would have thought "Great, we have been publicly humiliated, beaten, chained up, and put in jail. We are trying our best to still praise You, God, and this is how you thank us?"

Have you ever been in a situation like this? Have you gone through a hard time in your life, trying your best to praise God and follow Him, yet an earthquake still came? If so, write about it below.

God used the *violent earthquake* to free them from their chains. Not so that they could escape, but the life of the jailer could be saved along with his whole household!

Has God used an *earthquake* in your life to free you from a hard situation or a sin? If so, write about it below.

Did you see this freedom as just an escape from the situation or sin? Or did you use this new freedom to help lead others to Christ?

According to Acts 16:33–34, how were Paul and Silas taken care of by the jailer?

Check all that apply:

o   Their wounds were washed
o   They were welcomed into his house
o   A meal was set before them
o   They told them a story

Have you ever felt humiliated, beaten, or persecuted for following Jesus? If so, write about it below.

My friends, hard times will come to all of us, *but* God takes care of His children. Right now, you might be in the middle of a beating, imprisonment, or in an earthquake, *but* God will take care of you. It is interesting to me that the jailer took care of their basic needs. He washed their wounds, gave them shelter and food. When hard times come, we do not need to worry because God will always take care of us.

How did the magistrates react when they found out that Paul and Silas were Roman citizens? What actions did the magistrates take?

The magistrates realized that they were in big trouble. When Paul and Silas were brought in front of them, the magistrates did not listen to them but instead they listened to the crowd and the owners of the slave girl. There should have been a trail. Now, they have beaten Roman citizens. This was such a serious mistake that if word had gotten back to Roman Philippi, he could have lost his status as a Roman Colony.

What did they tell Paul and Silas to do? What did Paul do before leaving Philippi?

They were in so much trouble that the magistrates wanted them to leave fast. But Paul and Silas knew that they were not going to harm them anymore, which is why they were not in a hurry.

Read Paul's words in Romans 8:35–39.

Paul asks the question in verse 35, "Who can separate us from the love of God?" and then he questions if seven different things can separate us from the love of God. List them below.

Which of these things did Paul have happen to him while in Philippi?

Now, write Romans 8:37–39.

With God's love and strength, you can conquer anything you face in this world! Paul did not forget this important truth. When you feel beaten and humiliated by this world, remember that God is still with you. I hope that today's lesson encouraged you. I know it encouraged me. If you are looking for more encouragement, you will be happy to come back next week when we start the book of Philippians! But don't forget about our review day tomorrow!

Week One, Day Five:
Week in Review

Please begin with prayer. Pray that God will open your heart, speak to you, help you understand this scripture, show you how to apply these truths, and give you the power to apply His Word to your life.

On the space below, write out your Bible verse for this week. Then, spend at least five minutes analyzing the scripture. Refer to day one so you can remember what you need to be looking.

_____

_____

_____

_____

_____

_____

_____

_____

_____

_____

_____

_____

I want you to go back and reread Acts 9:1–21 and reread Acts chapter 16. Then, without looking back on your notes, try to summarize what you learned from these passages. What did you learn about God's character from these passages? Did God specifically tell you to do something this week? Write your review and answers down. After you do this, go back and flip through the week and make any extra notes of things you forgot but you want to make sure you don't forget next time you read these passages.

_____

_____

_____

_____

_____

_____

_____

_____

_____

_____

_____

_____

_____

_____

_____

_____

_____

_____

_____

_____

_____

_____

Small Group Questions

1. Refer to your review day, and take turns sharing with your group your summary of what happened in the Scriptures you read this week.

2. What did God specifically teach you this week? Did God tell you to do something specific this week? Did you learn something new about God's character? If you need to, refer to the review day and take turns sharing with the group.

3. Share with each other areas that you are struggling with that you need prayer. Do not be scared to open up and share. God wants us to lift each other up in prayer. Ask for prayer that God will help you with anything He has told you to do. Write down everyone's prayer requests, and commit to praying for your friends during the week when you do this study. End your time together by praying specifically for each request.

_____

_____

_____

_____

_____

_____

_____

_____

_____

_____

_____

_____

_____

_____

_____

Week Two M and M Bible Verses

Please pick one Bible verse to meditate on this week and memorize. Remember, you can pick a different translation.

"Being confident of this that he who began a good work in you will carry it on to completion until the day of Christ Jesus" (Phil. 1:6).

"And this is my prayer: that your love may abound more and more in knowledge and depth of insight, so that you may be able to discern what is best and may be pure and blameless for the day of Christ" (Phil. 1:9–10).

"For to me, to live is Christ and to die is gain" (Phil. 1:21).

"Whatever happens, conduct yourselves in a manner worthy of the Gospel of Christ. Then, whether I come and see you or only hear about you in my absence, I will know that you stand firm in the one Spirit, striving together as one for the faith of the gospel" (Phil. 1:27).

"Do nothing out of selfish ambition or vain conceit. Rather, in humility value others above yourselves, not looking to your own interests but each of you to the interests of the others" (Phil. 2:3–4).

Week Two, Day One: A Greeting from Paul

Start today with prayer. Pray that God will open your heart, speak to you, help you understand this scripture, show you how to apply these truths, and give you the power to apply His Word to your life.

On the space below, write out your Bible verse for this week. Then, spend at least five minutes analyzing the scripture. Refer to day one so you can remember what you need to be looking for.

_____

_____

_____

_____

_____

_____

_____

_____

_____

_____

_____

_____

_____

Paul wrote his letter to the church in Philippi while he was in prison. There is some debate on which imprisonment Paul was in during this time, but the important thing to note is that Paul was in prison. Paul wrote his letter to the church in Philippi as a thank you for sending him financial support and encouragement.

Read Phil. 1:1–2 and write it out.

When I read this passage, my mind went to so many places. First, I noted that Paul added Timothy in with his name. How awesome is that! I can't imagine having my name added right beside such a hero of the faith. Not only that, but Paul says both him and Timothy are bond servants of Christ Jesus! So often, we elevate people to high positions in the faith above us or we think we are better than others, but in reality, we should *all* be bond servants together.

The Greek word for *bond servant* can also be translated as *slave*. A slave or servant in this context was someone who lived "to serve his or her master." They really had no life outside of their service to their master. They had a very low status, and could only be elevated by their master.

What do you think it means to be a servant or slave for Christ?

To whom did Paul write his letter?

I love that Paul uses the phrase "to all the saints in Christ Jesus." Paul did not just say, "To all of the Church members." No, he called them saints in Christ Jesus! I read one commentary that said Paul "refers to the whole body of Christians as the holy people of God, set apart for Him in Christ."

If Paul wrote a letter to you personally today, do you think he would call you a saint, or someone who is holy and set apart for Christ?

I have to be honest and say that some days Paul might be able to say that about me, but other days, not so much. But that is where grace comes in!

Paul also addresses the letter to the overseers and deacons. I think Paul specifically set them apart in his greeting because he wanted to thank them as much as the whole church. Paul most likely realized that these leaders had a role in helping collect the money that the church sent Paul, and Paul wanted to make sure that he thanked them.

When I read the phrase *bond servant*, I remembered that James also calls himself a *bond servant* in his book of the Bible. This made me go on a search in all of Paul's greetings in the many letters he wrote that ended up in the New Testament. I want you to read the following greetings, and fill in the information under each section. I will fill in the first one for you.

Who was the letter written to? What did Paul call himself? How did Paul greet them?

1. *Philippians 1:1–2*

> Overseers, deacons, and saints in Philippi
> bond servant   Grace and Peace

2. *Ephesians 1:1–2*

3. *Colossians 1:1–2*

4. *Titus 1:1–4*

Paul sometimes calls himself a bond servant and sometimes he calls himself an apostle, but what was the same in each of these passages?

In all of Paul's letters, he always wished grace and peace to his audience in his greeting. Paul wished grace on them because of the new hope and grace that we only have through Jesus. When Paul used the word *peace*, he was saying "Shalom" which was the way that the Jews greeted each other and wished peace to each other in the Old Testament.

Paul realized how important it is to look at new things God reveals to us (grace from Christ Jesus), but Paul also wanted to connect the new things he was learning with the old ways, also (peace from God the Father).

How can you make sure you are remembering what God has taught you in the past and still connect them with what God is showing you right now?

Paul was also simply wishing grace and peace to them. I love grace and peace. How would you define biblical grace and peace?

I would define grace as something that we receive but we do not deserve. We do not deserve salvation, yet God gives it to us and we cannot do anything to earn it. Jesus has earned it for us. Jesus offers it to us as a free gift. Grace continues after we become Christians. When we sin, God still loves us and offers grace and forgiveness.

Have you accepted God's gift of grace? If so, how does knowing that God's grace still covers your sins today encourage you?

Do you have a sin you are struggling with right now that you need to ask forgiveness for and receive God's grace? If so, write about it below.

I would define peace as something that we all long for in troubled times. I am sure we have all had hard times in our lives when we seem to have no hope. When Jesus comes into our lives, He offers us peace for our minds and hearts.

Is there an area in your life where you long for peace? If so, write about it below. Then, pray and ask God to help give you peace in this area. (We will talk more about this the last week of our study.)

We need both grace and peace that can only come from Jesus Christ. I am glad that Paul takes the time to remind us of this in the very beginning of his letter.

Week Two, Day Two: Paul Remembers Philippi

Start today with prayer. Pray that God will open your heart, speak to you, help you understand this scripture, show you how to apply these truths, and give you the power to apply His Word to your life. Make sure you add in the pray requests your group shared.

On the space below, write out your Bible verse for this week. Then, spend at least five minutes analyzing the scripture. Refer to day one so you can remember what you need to be looking for.

_____
_____
_____
_____
_____
_____
_____
_____
_____
_____
_____
_____
_____
_____

I love the word *all* in the Bible. Each time I read it, I think "Not part of but *all*." Go ahead and read Philippians 1:3–7. Paul says, "I thank my God in all my remembrance of you." He didn't thank God part of the time for them, Paul thanked God *all* the time.

What other phrases do you see in this passage that tells you Paul prayed for them often?

The passage we are reading today shows us how much Paul loved the people in Philippi. We see in this passage that Paul often thought of them, and when he thought of them, he prayed for them with joy.

Right now, we have a team from my church on a mission trip and a group of kids at camp. I promised both groups that I would be praying for them while they were gone. I do have a set time a day that I pray when I spend time with my Lord, but I am trying to get into the habit of saying short prayers for people when I think of them. This week, I might be cleaning up my house, making lunch, running an errand, sitting down to eat a snack, or watching TV. I think of both of these groups of people and I either stop what I am doing and I pray for them, or I say a prayer for them while I am still doing what I am doing. I think this might be close to what Paul was talking about when he said that he *always* offered prayer for the people of Philippi. When Paul wrote this letter, he was not with them and did not know when he would see them again. I think he missed them.

Reread the whole passage again, and write down all the emotional language that shows how much Paul cared for them.

According to verses 4 and 5, what was the reason that Paul had so much joy when he prayed for this body of believers?

Paul saw how much they participated in the spreading of the Gospel. Paul saw this when he was with them when they sent him gifts to help his ministry (even after Paul had left them), and Paul continued to see them work to spread the Gospel. I believe that Paul was proud of them. They brought joy to him because they were spreading the Gospel.

Read verses 6–7 again.

I have always loved verse 6. It has always encouraged me as a believer in Christ. How does this verse encourage you?

As I have been studying this book of the Bible and learning more about the close relationship that Paul had with this church, I started to read this verse differently. If Paul missed them and longed to see them again, I think he was trying to encourage himself in writing this verse to them. I think Paul might have been reminding himself that even if he missed them and wanted to be close to them (to help them grow), it wasn't Paul who saved them and he was not who they truly needed. They had God, and God was going to make sure that the work *he* began in them would be finished in the end.

Have you ever had to send a child to school and you worried that they would not remember all that you taught them? Has God ever moved you from one ministry to another, and you missed and worried about the people that you used to minister to? How does this verse now encourage you if you look at it from Paul's viewpoint?

Paul had a very close bond with this church, and he says in verse 7 that there is nothing wrong with him feeling this way. Paul even uses the phrase "I have you in my heart" which shows how close Paul was with them.

Fill in the blanks (verse 7, I am using the NASB).

"Since both in my _____ and in the _____ and _____ of the gospel, you all are partakers of grace with me."

The church in Philippi never forgot Paul. They helped him while he was in prison, and now they were helping him get ready for his defense in court in hopes that Paul would be able to share the Gospel with more people. No wonder Paul had such love for these people! I wish I could say that as Christians today, we live like the church in Philippi—supporting ministers and missionaries *all* of the time. And *not forgetting them*. I think, too often in America, we get busy with our everyday lives and we forget that there are ministries and missionaries that need our help. We need to be involved to help spread the Gospel. We need to physically be the hands and feet of Jesus in our community, and we also need to be helping missionaries.

Could a minister or missionary write to you and say "I thank my God in all my remembrance of you... in view of your participation in the gospel from the first day until now... I have you in my

47

heart, since both in my imprisonment and in the defense and confirmation of the gospel, you all are partakers of grace with me."

I want to be a partaker of grace. I want to spread the Gospel and help others spread the Gospel. Do you feel the same way? I hope you do!

Read Phil. 1:9–11.

Verse 9 says, "And this I pray, that your _____ may abound still more and more" (New American Standard).

When I first read this, I asked myself, "Why did Paul pray for their *love* to abound more and more, why not their faith or something else?" Then, I remembered that Paul was just thanking them for being partakers with him to help spread the Gospel. They were already showing love to Paul and the people around them, but Paul wanted their love to "abound still more and more." Paul knew that this was a strength that they had, and he prayed that this strength would continue to grow stronger.

Read Gal. 5:22–23. What is the first fruit of the Spirit that is listed?

Read 1 Cor. 13:1–3.

According to this passage, without _____ we are _____.

I also believe that Paul knew that love is the key to spreading the Gospel.

What did Paul want their love to grow in?

1.

2.

Where do we gain more knowledge about God?

The Greek word used for *discernment* here means "to test, examine, approve, or find out."

I believe that we gain more knowledge of what love is when we study God's Word deeply. I think that if we are going to test, discern, or examine how to love, we need to be listening to the Holy Spirit guiding us. In today's culture, it is sometimes hard to understand how to love people who are different from us. We need knowledge and discernment from God. We need to be listening to the Holy Spirit telling us what to do.

Read 1 John 3:16 and write it down below.

Jesus is love and is the best example of love for us to look to. To be able to love others, we must know and have a close relationship with Jesus first so we can then love others the same way Jesus loves us. To have a close relationship with Jesus, we need to learn to hear His Spirit talking to us every day.

According to this passage, what will we be able to do if our love abounds in knowledge and discernment?

There are things in life that are clearly bad choices and good choices. When you choose to steal something, it is clearly a bad choice. It is a good choice to be involved in helping with a ministry or spreading the Gospel. But when it comes to ministry, sometimes we do not stop to seek God's Word and the Holy Spirit to see if what we want to do is really the *best* (or superior) thing to do. It might be a good thing. It might be fun, but is it the *best* way to spread the Gospel and share the love of Christ?

Check off all of the reasons why a church might have a ministry or event *other* than God leading them to do this ministry or event:

- o   Other churches have done this and been successful
- o   It is a tradition of your church
- o   It will be fun
- o   _____ (fill in with any other reason you can think of)

I am convinced that we need to seek God to find the *best*, more *excellent*, or *superior* way that God wants us to use His money and His people to spread the good news of the Gospel.

According to verse 10, why should we want to pick the best, more excellent, or superior way?

Read 2 Corinthians 5:10. What will all Christians one day have to do?

The word used for *pure* here means "to hold something under light to be able to see it better." This made me think of the envelope trick. You know if you ever get something in the mail for someone else in your family and you want to know what it is, you hold it up to the light to see if you can make out any of the words. We should be so pure that even if we might look good on the outside, when light is shined on us, people will see that what is inside us (our true nature) still looks pure I don't know about you, but when I stand before God, I want to be pure and blameless. I want to be able to say to God that I did my *best* to love others for Him, and that I wasn't just following tradition. I do not want to just look good on the outside. I want God's Word in my heart so I can better hear the Holy Spirit guide me in every area of my life. Then, I will be "filled with the fruit of righteousness which comes through Jesus Christ" (Phil.1:11). I can't live this life on my own. I need to be filled with Christ's righteousness if I want to love others and make a difference for Him.

Do you feel the same way? Think about it.

End today by praying and asking God to give you a desire to be pure and blameless. Pray that He will show you how you can grow closer to Him, and that He will show you how to love others more and more every day.

Week Two, Day Three:
Paul Answers a Question

Please pray before you begin. Please do not forget to pray for the requests your group shared.

On the space below, write out your Bible verse for this week. Then, spend at least five minutes analyzing the scripture.

_____
_____
_____
_____
_____
_____
_____
_____
_____
_____
_____
_____
_____
_____
_____
_____

My kids ask me questions all the time. Sometimes they are easy to answer, other times not so much. Like when my daughter asks me, "What makes people die?" That was a fun one to answer. Today, we are going to be studying a passage in Philippians where Paul answers a question or was trying to clear up some kind of misunderstanding.

Read Philippians 1:12. How does Paul start this verse?

Paul uses the phrase "I want you to know" in other letters that he wrote. Each time he says this, he is either responding to a question that he was asked or he was trying to clear up a misunderstanding.

Knowing this, what question do you think the church in Philippi asked or what was Paul trying to help them understand?

The church could have shown concern for Paul being in jail. They might have thought that he did not need to be in jail, and they might have asked Paul how he was handling being in jail.

Think back to our first two days of background in the Book of Acts. Write down what you remember happened to Paul while he was in jail in Philippi.

The church in Philippi knew that Paul had been in tough situations before and this was not the first time he had been in jail, but what is the main difference between what happened in Philippi and what was happening to Paul right then?

Read 1:13. Why did Paul say he was still in prison?

Paul had not escaped jail this time, but just like God used his jail time in Philippi to save the jailer and his household, God was using Paul in jail again to spread the Gospel.

The Christians in Philippi might have been showing concern for Paul because this time he had not escaped. They might have questioned why God would want Paul to be in jail for so long. They loved Paul and did not understand what was going on.

Have you ever questioned God when He did not respond to a situation the same way He had in the past? Have you ever questioned God when He did not respond to your situation the same way He had with someone else who was going through the same situation? If so, write about the situation below.

How does Phil. 1:13 encourage you?

Read Phil. 1:14. What great things came as a result of Paul's imprisonment?

Paul was in jail, but the Gospel was being spread and more Christians were having the courage to share the Gospel. It might have been hard for Paul to be in jail, but God was using this hard situation to bring about *great* things! I recently read a story of a family who lived in a country where Christians are watched very closely by the government. Each time this family shared Christ with others in their city, they were then asked to leave not only their home but also the city. These Christians were persecuted for telling others about Jesus. The government thought they would discourage this family, but instead, they helped this family spread the Gospel even more. Each time the family shared Christ with a group of people, they were asked to leave. This happened seven times, and each time, they started a new church in the city they left. They might be persecuted, but God is using their persecution to bring about great things!

Has God ever used a hard situation in your life to help spread the Gospel or to give you more courage in spreading the Gospel? If so, write about it below.

Now read Phil. 1:15–18. Two groups of people started preaching Christ as a result of Paul's imprisonment. Write down all of the descriptions given for each group.

Preaching out of envy and strife   Preaching from good will

Do you try to reach more people for Christ so you can say that you have a bigger number of people who go to your church? Is it really about reaching people with the love of Christ, or is it so you or your church can look good? Please search your heart and write down your honest answer.

Have you ever been joyous about another ministry or church? Have you ever wanted to outshine that ministry or church? If so, write about the situation below.

I feel that I should add something in here. As a minister's wife, it is very tempting to look at other churches and get discouraged when they are growing but your church or ministry is not. It is tempting to get jealous. I have done this many times before. We should all realize that we are all trying to spread the Gospel, and even if you might not agree with all of that *other church's* methods, we should still seek to support them and not be jealous of them. When we are jealous, we say bad things about the other group, and that is not what Christ would want. End of my story. Back to the scripture.

I pray that you want to reach people so you can share the love of Christ with them and not so your group can look better from other people's perspective. There is good news if you have not been reaching people with the right motive. Read Phil. 1:18.

No matter our motives, God speaks to the hearts of people when His Gospel is shared! Even if we mess up and are only doing ministry to look good in front of others, God can use His message to reach people! I believe that we should always check our motives, but it is nice to know that when the Word of God is taught that He is the one who works in the hearts of men, not us.

How does this encourage you today?

Week Two, Day Four: "To Live Is Christ and to Die Is Gain"

Please begin today with prayer. Don't forget to pray for the requests your group shared.

On the space below, write out your Bible verse for this week. Then, spend at least five minutes analyzing the scripture.

_____

_____

_____

_____

_____

_____

_____

_____

_____

_____

_____

_____

_____

_____

If you have not realized yet, Philippians is one of my all-time favorite books of the Bible. It has so many great encouraging passages in it, and today we are going to be studying a passage that I believe is very well known but one that some believers might be scared to study. *We* are not going to be scared. Say it with me, "I am not going to be scared away by today's study!" Now, we are ready to start.

Read Phil. 1:19–20.

"For I know that this will turn out for my _____" (Phil. 1:19 NASB).

The word that is used here can be used as deliverance from a dangerous situation on earth, or being delivered from your sins into eternal salvation. The commentaries I read said that Paul could have used this word to mean that he was looking forward to his deliverance from jail, or he could have been using it in a broader sense to mean that no matter what happened to him in the end, he would be delivered because he would end up in heaven with his Lord and Savior. I'm not sure how Paul meant to use this word *deliverance*. Maybe he meant it in both ways, maybe just one way. I do think that it is important to note that we all need deliverance! Maybe it is from a hard situation here on this earth or maybe it is from something spiritual you are struggling with.

Do you need to be delivered from anything today? If so, write about it below.

What two things helped in Paul's deliverance according to verse 19?

Paul gained strength from the prayers that were offered for him and from the Holy Spirit of Jesus Christ. Isn't it great to know that we can pray for others to be strengthened and that God will use his Holy Spirit to strengthen them? I think that often people go through situations that I have never had to face and I don't know what to say to them. I do know that God is there for them, and that the comfort they will receive from the Holy Spirit will far surpass anything I could say to them. From now on, when I don't know what to say or do, I will at least make it a point to pray and ask God to comfort them with His Holy Spirit and to guide me on anything else I can do to help.

Who can you go to and ask to pray for you about what you need to be delivered from?

Read Phil. 1:20. What did Paul *not* want to happen?

What did Paul want to happen?

I think that we will all agree that we would love to be bolder for Christ and to bring Him more honor.

Write out verse 21 below:

This is a hard verse to read. It is hard to imagine that to die would be a gain.

Read Phil. 1:21–26.

What two places was Paul having a hard time choosing between?

In verse 23, Paul says that he has "the desire to depart and be with Christ, for that is very much better." I once asked a woman (who is married and has young children) how she was able to have hope while having cancer. She told me that she realized if she died, she would win because she would get to go to heaven. If she lived, she would win because she could stay with her family longer. She said it was win-win in her eyes. Paul was so close to Christ and wanted to follow Him so much that both death and life had positive aspects.

Could you say that today? Are you close enough to Christ that if you had to leave this world you would see it as a win? If not, what is making you want to stay on this earth? Are you closer to that thing or person than you are to Christ?

I want to be that close to Christ.

According to Phil. 1:24–26, what did Paul chose?

I think that Paul wanted to be there for his friends, and even if he longed to go to heaven to be with his Lord and Savior, he knew that he still had work to do on earth.

My husband laughs at me because, up until a few months ago, I *never* read books. Now, I love to read books. I am so hungry to hear from God that not only am I reading my Bible more, but I am reading books by different Christian authors on how to grow as a Christian. Today, I was reading the book *Follow Me* by David Platt. In this section of the book, he was talking about Jesus and heaven. He tells a story of a young man who was dying of cancer, and David went to visit him in the hospital. When he got there to visit this young man (who was married and had a child), the man was not sad that he was dying. Instead, he looked at David and said, "I'm going to be with Jesus today." David then goes on to quote Philippians 1:21 (you wrote this verse down earlier). As I read this, I cried. I read this the same day I was writing this day of the Bible study. I love how God does things like that. We do not need to think that *only* Paul can have that close of a relationship with God. We can, too.

My prayer is that we will all be that close to Christ.

What about you? Do you see the work that God has for you? Do you see how God wants to continue to use you?

Pray and ask God to show you what He wants you to be involved with. Seek out having that close of a relationship with God like Paul had. It can happen.

Below, write out your prayer to God asking Him to show you where He wants to use you (I know we have already done this, but please do it again if you do not have an answer yet) and be bold enough to ask God to help you have a close enough relationship with Him that you can honestly say Phil. 1:21 and mean it.

Week Two, Day Five: Week in Review

Today, I want you to begin with prayer (like all of the rest of the days). Pray that God will open your heart, speak to you, help you understand this scripture, show you how to apply these truths, and give you the power to apply His Word to your life. Make sure you pray for the requests that your group shared.

On the space below, write out your Bible verse for this week. Then, spend at least five minutes analyzing the scripture.

_____

_____

_____

_____

_____

_____

_____

_____

_____

_____

_____

_____

_____

_____

I want for you to go back and reread Phil. 1:1–26. Then, without looking back on your notes, try to summarize what you learned from these passages. What did you learn about God's character from these passages? Did God specifically tell you to do something this week? Write your review and answers down. After you do this, go back and flip through the week and make any extra notes of things you forgot but you want to make sure you don't forget next time you read these passages.

Small Group Questions

1. Refer to your review day and take turns sharing with your group your summary of what happened in the Scriptures you read this week.

2. What did God specifically teach you this week? Did God tell you to do something specific this week? Did you learn something new about God's character? If you need to, refer to the review day and take turns sharing with the group.

3. Share with each other areas that you are struggling with that you need prayer. Do not be scared to open up and share. God wants us to lift each other up in prayer. Ask for prayer that God will help you with anything He has told you to do. Write down everyone's prayer requests, and commit to praying for your friends during the week when you do this study. End your time together by praying specifically for each request.

_____
_____
_____
_____
_____
_____
_____
_____
_____
_____
_____
_____
_____
_____

Week Three M and M Bible Verses

"In your relationships with one another, have the same mindset as Christ Jesus" (Phil. 2:5).

"And being found in appearance as a man, he humbled himself by becoming obedient to death—even death on a cross" (Phil. 2:8).

"Therefore, my dear friends, as you have always obeyed—not only in my presence, but now much more in my absence—continue to work out your salvation with fear and trembling, for it is God who works in you to will and to act in order to fulfill his good purpose" (Phil. 2:12–13).

"Do everything without grumbling or arguing, 15 so that you may become blameless and pure, 'children of God without fault in a warped and crooked generation.' Then you will shine among them like stars in the sky" (Phil. 2:14–15).

"Do not store up for yourselves treasures on earth, where moths and vermin destroy, and where thieves break in and steal. But store up for yourselves treasures in heaven, where moths and vermin do not destroy, and where thieves do not break in and steal. For where your treasure is, there your heart will be also" (Matt. 6:19–21).

Week Three, Day One:
Whatever Happens…

Please begin today with prayer. Don't forget to pray for the requests your group shared.

On the space below, write out your Bible verse for this week. Then, spend at least five minutes analyzing the scripture.

_____

_____

_____

_____

_____

_____

_____

_____

_____

_____

_____

_____

_____

_____

_____

_____

_____

Yesterday we talked about how Paul was close enough to Christ that he saw dying as a positive thing. Fresh off this passage, Paul tells the church how they should conduct themselves. In one translation, it says that Paul started by saying "Whatever happens… " I read this and I thought of a scene in a movie where a hero is giving life or death instructions to someone else, and then before they leave, they say something like "You might hear a lot of noise out here, you might even hear gunshots, but no matter what you hear, I want you to stay in this room! Whatever happens, you need to stay in here!" Can you picture a scene like that? Scenes like this happen in the movies because they know that the character is going to be tempted to not follow their instructions, so that is why they are told "Whatever happens… "

Read Phil. 1:27–30.

Paul wanted them to conduct themselves in a manner worthy of what?

The words here used for conduct and manner were both connected with the military. So when Paul told them to "conduct yourselves in a manner worthy of the Gospel of Christ," they would have associated this with being dedicated Roman citizens. Paul knew that many of the people living in Philippi were military veterans, but Paul was calling them to be more than just dedicated Roman citizens or dedicated veterans. Paul wanted them to make sure that they realize they also have a citizenship with Christ!

Paul wanted to hear that they were _____ _____ in one spirit. (Verse 27)

This image of *standing firm* goes right back to the military, and Paul is also using the image of an athletic team. Paul knew that both the military and an athletic team were untied for certain goals and they worked together to meet those goals. Paul wanted the church to be untied to help spread the gospel.

How else did Paul want for them to be unified? (Verse 27)

Would you say that your church stands "firm in one spirit, with one mind striving together for the faith of the gospel?"

A lot of issues can arise in a church. In my own church within the past year, we have had debates on women deacons, the music ministry, should the church hire a full*time music minister, the youth ministry, and what are we going to do about the people leaving our church. This is just the church that I attend, but I think that we are not alone in our lack of unity. I think it is important to note that having *one spirit* and *one mind* and standing firm side by side in the church is so we can better understand and share the Gospel. We will not always get along on every issue, but I think it is important that we make sure that our main goal in our churches is the Great Commission.

Read Matthew 28:18–20. According to this passage, what should be the church's main goal that our *one spirit* and *one mind* should revolve around?

How is your church doing this well?

How is your church *not* doing this well?

How can *you* help bring unity to your church and help spread the Gospel?

Back to our passage. Read Phil. 1:28. What should they not be alarmed by?

The outside world saw persecution as something that should destroy the church. Paul wanted them to be unified so they could stand against persecution and make it through the persecution. Persecution made the church stronger, and when the outside world saw that these Christians were willing to die for their faith in Christ, the world then realized that the Christians must have been following something that was worth learning more about.

Write down verse Phil. 1:29.

In this verse, it talks about how persecution was *granted* or *given* to the church as if this was a gift or an honor that was given to the church. I read this verse and I thought again about all of the military references in this passage. I thought about an honor being given to someone who served his country, or how a military man would consider it an honor to be hurt in service to his country.

It is clear to me that if you are doing this Bible study that you must believe in Christ, but do you also believe that persecution is a blessing granted to you?

In preparation for this Bible study, I have read many stories of Christians being persecuted for their faith. I read stories of Christians being put in jail for many years. They had to leave their families, and they were tortured beyond words. Many of them were killed for believing in Christ.

Would you still follow Christ even if you knew you could be put in jail (away from your family) and tortured?

I hope that I would be able to stay strong during such persecution.

Many churches in America today are choosing not to stand on what the Bible clearly says is wrong and right. They are being pressured by the world to change what they believe, and for the sake of unity within the church body (and unity with the world), these churches are willing to change what they believe. This is not real unity! We need to be of the same mind, standing firm on the Word of God. If our one mind is not coming from the Word of God, then it is wrong. Our churches should not try to be unified with the world's standards no matter what persecution may come. If we do not stand firm on the Word of God, then we will not be able to show the world God's love and how He wants them to live.

So imagine Christ (our hero) standing before your church, and He tells you, "Hard times are going to come. You are not always going to agree on everything and you will be persecuted. You will want to leave. You will be scared. *But* whatever happens, I want for you to stand together and be of one mind and one spirit so you can better know and spread the Gospel to the world!" I hope this encourages you today!

Week Three, Day Two:
Unity and the Golden Rule

Please begin with prayer. Don't forget to pray for the requests your group shared.

On the space below, write out your Bible verse for this week. Then, spend at least five minutes analyzing the scripture.

_____

_____

_____

_____

_____

_____

_____

_____

_____

_____

_____

_____

_____

_____

_____

_____

We ended yesterday talking about unity. Our passage today starts off with the word *therefore*, so we know that Paul is going to continue to talk about unity, and he is connecting what he is about to say to what he just said. Today, we will read yesterday's passage along with today's passage. Let's read Phil. 1:27–2:4.

Write down the four *if* statements in verse 2:1.

1.

2.

3.

4.

All four of these things are blessings that we, as Christians, gain from Christ and from being involved in our church. I should note, *the spirit* in this verse is talking about the Holy Spirit. Which of these four things have you felt the most in your church?

Paul then goes on to say in verse 2, "make my _____ complete by being of the same _____" (NASB).

Paul said already that he wants to hear good news about what the church in Philippi is doing. Now, he wants his joy to be complete for them. Paul tells them they can make his joy complete by having the same mind. Paul then goes on to explain how they can have the same mind.

What three things does Paul tell them to do so they can make sure they are of the same mind? Please note the translation below so it will be easier to talk about.

"Make my joy complete by being of the same mind, maintaining the same love, united in spirit, intent on one purpose" (Phil. 2:2 NASB).

1.

2.

3.

How can we make sure we are maintaining the same love?

How can we be united with the Holy Spirit? Both personally and in our church.

What should be the churches' one purpose that we are intent on, and how do we make sure we are intent on it?

Now, read verses 2:3–4. What should we *not* do? What should we do?

And once again, we have come across a word that we have already heard in this letter. The word is *selfish* (or selfishness as it is used here). Which group did Paul use this same word to describe in week two, day three?

Selfish ambition was used to describe the people in Phil. 1:17 that were preaching Christ out of envy and strife. I think Paul might have still been thinking about this group of people when Paul used the word selfishness again. Paul wanted to make sure that the people in the church at Philippi were not focusing on themselves and only looking out for themselves.

Paul also calls them to be something that the people in the church would not have seen as a good thing.

"But with _____ of mind regard one another as more important than yourselves" (verse 3).

Humility. According to Dictionary.com, the word *humility* is a noun and it is defined as "the quality or condition of being humble; modest opinion or estimate of one's own importance, rank, etc." Synonyms for the word *humility* include "lowliness, meekness, and submissiveness." An antonym for the word *humility* is *pride*. For the most part, I think that people in our culture today would want to be known as a humble person. But back when Paul wrote this, the word for humility was used to describe slaves, and it showed that slaves were *unfit people*. Paul has already tried to get them to see themselves as slaves, and now he is saying that they should also think of themselves in the same way that a slave does. Go back to week one, day five and read again my description of a slave.

Paul was telling them that they should *live* for serving others and put others' needs before their own. Yes, they needed to look out for their own *personal interests* so Paul was not telling them to not take care of themselves, but Paul wanted them to purposely serve others and put their needs before themselves.

Can you think of a time when someone else has put their needs on hold to help you? How did this make you feel? Write about it below.

Has anyone in your church put your needs before their own? If so, write about it below.

On a scale of one to ten, how often do you put other people's needs in your church (outside of your family) before your own needs?

Now, let's remember that this passage of scripture is with a section of scripture where Paul is talking about church unity. We need to remember that church is not about us. Many Christians see church as a place where they should be served, but actually, the opposite is true. Christians should be going to church to serve others. Yes, we will be able to worship with other believers and we will hopefully feel closer to Christ when we leave our weekly church meetings. But we should not be going to church every week only so other people encourage us or serve us. Instead, we should be going to church and be looking for ways to serve and encourage other believers. If every Christian put the needs of other church members before their own, this would cut out a lot of disunity.

How do you think putting the needs of others before your self would help when your church is involved with a sensitive topic that is causing disunity?

If we have a "modest opinion or estimate of one's own importance," do you think this would help you put the needs of others before your own when dealing with a sensitive topic that is causing disunity?

I think that if we are really being humble and putting the needs of our fellow church members before our own, then when a sensitive topic comes up, we will discuss it with love and be more willing to find a common ground.

Do you think your opinions are more important than others? Can you think of a time when you thought your option was right and the other person's option was wrong? Write about it below.

I did not think that I had a problem with this until God showed me that a lot of times I think that I am on God's side on a topic and then everyone else is wrong. I tell myself that they just don't understand the Bible as well as I do. And to be honest, most of the subjects that cause disunity in churches are topics where scholars debate what the Bible says on that particular topic (once again, I am not talking about when the church is seeking unity with the world and making sin look like it is not really sin). But I seem to think that *my* view on the topic is right, and their view is wrong. I use God as an excuse for looking at others badly because they disagree with me. When, really, none of us are perfect. I am no better than anyone else. We all need God's grace. We are all spiritually on different levels, and God wants us to work together. God has shown me that I need to be more humble, and even if I believe my option lines up with God's word, I should not make someone else feel badly or cause my church to stop being involved with what really matters (reaching the lost and serving others) so we can handle an issue that is very small compared to the whole of the Gospel.

Is your church dealing with any issues right now that are causing disunity? If so, list them below.

After reading today's lesson, how can you humbly help bring church unity on at least one of these topics? Please pray and seek God's guidance on this question.

Week Three, Day Three: Christ, Our Ultimate Example!

Please begin today with prayer. Don't forget to pray for the requests your group shared.

On the space below, write out your Bible verse for this week. Then, spend at least five minutes analyzing the scripture.

_____

_____

_____

_____

_____

_____

_____

_____

_____

_____

_____

_____

_____

_____

Paul wraps up his talk about unity by telling the church to look toward Christ because He is the ultimate example of humility and servanthood.

Read Phil. 2:5–11.

What does Paul say in verse 5 that we should do?

Paul then goes on to quote a popular hymn from that day in Phil. 2:5–11. Paul used this hymn because it best described Jesus and helped Paul make the point he was trying to make! I never realized that this part of scripture was a hymn in the early church. I think it is interesting that Paul used a hymn to illustrate his point.

According to verse 7, what did Jesus do and become?

Jesus, the Son of God, had to empty Himself (some translations say that He became nothing), and become a slave for us. We need to be willing to be like Christ and be willing to empty ourselves. One way we can do this is by being willing to empty or rid ourselves of sin.

Read Eph. 4:22–32, 1 Peter 2:1, and Coll. 3:5–10, and write down what these passages say we should get rid of in our lives.

That is a great list of things we need to rid ourselves (and many are even repeated) of, but there are still things that are not on this list. What on this list do you need to empty yourself of so you can have an attitude like Christ? What is not on this list that you also need to empty yourself of so you can have an attitude like Christ? What is on this list that is going to be the hardest thing for you to get rid of?

How do you need to humble yourself so you can be obedient to Christ?

All of these questions are very hard to answer, so if you cannot answer them right now, please be thinking of them and meditate on this scripture so God can show you the answers.

The first part of this hymn (2:5–8) shows us how we, as a church, should have the same attitude of Jesus. The second part (2:9–11) focuses on who Christ is and why we should worship Him.

Now, I want for you to reread 2:9–11, then read Revelation 1:4–7. List the different ways Jesus is described in both of these passages.

<u>Phil. 2:9–11</u>   <u>Rev. 1:4–7</u>

After reading these passages, don't you want to just stop what you are doing and worship Jesus? Pause for just a little bit and take some time to praise Jesus for who He is and what He has done, not only for you but for all of mankind! Say a prayer or sing a song. Let this be a time of praise and thankfulness! Write any thoughts you have below.

Paul knew that in order for us to have the same attitude of Christ, we need to realize who Christ is and how much He deserves our praise. Then, we will want to have the same attitude as Jesus because this will be another way for us to praise Him! I think this is why Paul chose to use a hymn that the Church of Philippi would have known. Paul knew that when they sang this song, they would remember what Paul taught them. This song would have made them excited about Jesus's return, and would make them want to share Jesus with the people around them. My friends, Jesus is coming back! We should be excited about this, and this should make us want to share His love with more and more people.

Are you excited about Jesus's return?

What are you doing to make sure your friends and family members are ready for Jesus's return?

Week Three, Day Four: Christian's Obey God

We have so much to cover today, and this is one of those days where we have a harder topic to talk about, but it is important that we not pass over the topic of obedience. So, please do not forget to pray that God will open your heart and show you how you can live for Him and obey Him better in your daily life.

On the space below, write out your Bible verse for this week. Then, spend at least five minutes analyzing the scripture.

_____
_____
_____
_____
_____
_____
_____
_____
_____
_____
_____
_____
_____

Read Phil. 2:12.

What does Paul call them?

In some translations, Paul calls them his *beloved.* and in others, he calls them his *dear friends.* I think Paul knew that he was about to get serious with them and he needed to remind them that he loves them. I think that as Christians, we should try to follow Paul's example and make sure that we always tell people God's truth (which they might find very hard to follow) in love. We also need to be reminded as Christians that God does love us, *but* He also wants us to obey Him.

Let's take a side trip to some passages on obedience. Please read each passage and summarize them below.

I Sam. 15:22

John 14:5

Joshua 1:8

Deut. 10:12–13

If we want to be close to God and have a good relationship with Him, we *must* obey Him!

Go back and read Phil. 2:8.

"Being found in appearance as a man, He humbled Himself by becoming _____ to the point of death, even death on a cross" (NASB).

Christ is our ultimate example of humility and servanthood because He was obedient. If we want to be like Christ, we will obey God no matter what the cost.

Do you struggle with obeying God's Word on certain issues? If so, write about them below.

We also need to make sure that we are studying His Word and learning what God says about different issues. Then, we need to make sure we obey Him. We should love God so much that we are eager to learn His teachings and His commands, and then follow them. If we really want to obey God, we will not only obey Him, but as part of that obedience, we will be eager to learn His teachings so we can obey Him.

When you come across a teaching or command in the Bible that you don't agree with, what do you do?

It is important that we do not pick and choose parts of the Bible to follow. If we do not understand certain parts or teachings, then we must go to God and ask Him to help us understand. God will answer your prayer, but you must be willing to seek after Him.

Paul tells the Philippians that they were being obedient (especially when Paul was with them), but he wants to make sure that they are striving more and more to be obedient to Christ when Paul is not with them. It is easy to obey God when we are at church, Bible study, or youth group, but do we still act the same way when we are out in the real world? You don't have to answer that one. Just think about it.

Then, we come to a verse that I am sure will scare some Christians and just confuse other Christians.

What are we told to do at the end of Phil. 2:12?

When we become Christians, we are responsible to be obedient to God. I think Richard R. Melick best describes this passage in his commentary. He says, "Personal salvation brings with it responsibilities which Paul related to Christians' obedience. The responsibility was to live in accord with their salvation, letting the implications of their relationship with Christ transform their social relationships. Paul really meant, in the first place, that they were to act like Christians."

Outside of being a member of a local church, do you live your life in a way that the people around you would never question that you are a Christian?

Paul wanted to encourage the members of the Church of Philippi to live like Christians by obeying God. Being obedient to Christ in their everyday lives would show that they were really Christians and that they were truly saved. Therefore, if we ever question our salvation, we need to look at our lives and ask ourselves the question, "Am I following God and obeying His teachings and commands?" If the answer is *yes*, then there is no reason for doubt. If the answer is *no*, then we need to repent, turn from our sin, and start following God.

Some people might say, "But I know I am a Christian! I said a prayer when I was (insert age here)." But if we are not living our lives in obedience to Christ, we need to be willing to look at that time in our lives, and question if we really understood what we were doing. I am not talking about when we mess up and sin. We are not perfect. We will sin after we become Christians. But the difference is that we should not *want* to sin after we become Christians. Some people live a life of disobedience to God and it does not upset them that they are sinning. When asked if they are saved, they hang on to a prayer that they said when they were younger, yet they are fine with having sin in their life. There was never a real change in them. This is a problem. If we have truly been changed by Christ and He lives in us, we will want to obey Him.

Read Matthew 7:21–23. According to this passage, will everyone who claims to be a Christian really make it into heaven?

So if you are one of those people who thinks you might not have really understood or meant it when you prayed a prayer to become a Christian, don't be afraid to talk to someone. Be more concerned with what God thinks than what other people think. I have heard stories of many people who have grown up in church, walked an aisle, said a prayer, and were baptized. But then later, they realized that they were not really Christians.

Now, let us look at the phrase "with fear and trembling." Paul wanted the Philippians to have a respect for God. They (and we) need to respect God for who He is, and live our lives in reverence and awe of Him.

Read 1 Kings 18:16–39.

In verse 18, what did Elijah say that the people of Israel had abandoned?

If you had been there that day, what would you have thought of God? Would you have walked away with fear and respect for the one true God? Who would you have picked to follow after that day?

God wants us to live for Him and no one else. We do not need to abandon His commandments. He made them because He wants to take care of us. He can still do great and amazing things in our lives today, and He deserves our respect, but we have to pick Him and choose to follow His commands. Do you respect and fear God enough to follow Him in every area of your life? Think about that. I know today has been a hard day, but please do not be discouraged! Tomorrow, we are going to look at Phil. 2:13, and learn that, yes, we need to *work out* our salvation, but God is going to help us!

Week Three, Day Five: Week in Review

Today, I want for you to begin with prayer (like all of the rest of the days). Pray that God will open your heart, speak to you, help you understand this scripture, show you how to apply these truths, and give you the power to apply His Word to your life. Make sure you pray for the requests that your group shared.

On the space below, write out your Bible verse for this week. Then, spend at least five minutes analyzing the scripture.

_____

_____

_____

_____

_____

_____

_____

_____

_____

_____

_____

_____

I want for you to go back and reread Phil. 1:27–2:12. Also read Matthew 7:21–23, and 1 Kings 18:16–39. Then without looking back on your notes, try to summarize what you learned from these passages. What did you learn about God's character from these passages? Did God specifically tell you to do something this week? Write your review and answers down. After you do this, go back and flip through the week and make any extra notes of things you forgot but you want to make sure you don't forget next time you read these passages.

_____

_____

_____

_____

_____

_____

_____

_____

_____

_____

_____

_____

_____

_____

_____

_____

_____

_____

_____

_____

_____

Small Group Questions

1. Refer to your review day and take turns sharing with your group your summary of what happened in the Scriptures you read this week.

2. What did God specifically teach you this week? Did God tell you to do something specific this week? Did you learn something new about God's character? If you need to, refer to the review day and take turns sharing with the group.

3. Share with each other areas that you are struggling with that you need prayer. Do not be scared to open up and share. God wants us to lift each other up in prayer. Ask for prayer that God will help you with anything He has told you to do. Write down everyone's prayer requests, and commit to praying for your friends during the week when you do this study. End your time together by praying specifically for each request.

_____

_____

_____

_____

_____

_____

_____

_____

_____

_____

_____

_____

_____

_____

Week Four, Day One:
God is at Work in You!

Please begin with prayer.

On the space below, write out your Bible verse for this week. Then, spend at least five minutes analyzing the scripture.

_____
_____
_____
_____
_____
_____
_____
_____
_____
_____
_____
_____
_____
_____
_____
_____
_____

Yesterday, we talked about a verse that can be very confusing and hard to understand. But today, we are going to continue with the passage.

Read verse Phil. 2:13. What are we told that God is doing?

Many people might just read the end of verse 12, and not go on to read verse 13. Paul was painting a picture with his words. By using the words *work out* and *work in*, Paul was showing us that they both go hand in hand. By looking at verse 13, we see that God is at work in us! We *work out* our salvation and God will *work in* us! This means that God is going to *work in* us to give us the desire to obey Him and the ability to obey Him, *but* before God does those things, He will first *work in* us to call us to Him. Paul was calling these Christians (and us) to realize that our salvation is a gift from God, and we need to treat it with great care.

Read 1 Cor. 6:20, and write a summary below.

If we treat our gift of salvation as no big deal (and are not willing to obey God as a result of our salvation), then we will not shine for Jesus like we should.

There is another *work* in verse 13, what does this one say God will do?

God wants to use us to "work for His good pleasure." So, not only does our obedience to God give us the same attitude of Christ, brings us into a right relationship with God, and shows that we are truly saved, but it also makes us more available to God so He can use us to *work for* Him!

So, to sum it all up, God will *work in* us, and we will *work out* our salvation through obedience and, then God will use us to *work for* Him!

Now, read Phil. 2:14–15.

"Do _____ things without _____ or
_____ "

I bet you just love that verse! My translation says *grumbling and disputing*. Most translations have the first word as grumbling, but the second word is sometimes translated as complaining or arguing. This is a verse I have already memorized because I need to remember to do less complaining! Let us look at this verse in context of the passage it goes with.

According to verse 15, why should we follow verse 14?

Not only do we need to work out our salvation, but we also need to *prove* ourselves to be "blameless and innocent children of God," that are "above reproach" by doing "*all* things (emphasis mine) without grumbling or disputing." I don't think Paul was just using this as an example of one of the ways we can and should be obedient. Remember that Paul just spent a long time talking about how the church should be unified. I think Paul is using this as an example because, yes, personally we all need to follow this teaching. But churches need to follow this teaching, as well. If we want to personally be the light of Christ (and want your church to be the light of

Christ) to *a crooked and perverse generation*, then we need to not be complaining and grumbling within ourselves as church members.

Is there an area, ministry, or church member that you like to complain about? You do not have to write down names, but describe the situation as best as you can below.

How can you lead by example and *not* complain or grumble about that area, ministry, or church member?

Now that you have looked at yourself, let us look at your church as a group. We have already talked about how the church should be unified. So thinking back on those lessons and this lesson, how do you think you can encourage your church members to not grumble and complain/argue?

Along with not complaining yourself, one way you can help is to not let people complain to you. I know this might be hard. I have started trying to do this in my own life and it is *hard*, but I think it is worth it! If someone wants to complain to you, then lovingly tell them that you do not want to help spread disunity.

I understand that some issues in churches are hard to resolve. We will not always agree on everything. But we can and should agree that the purpose of the church is to be a place where we can worship God together, and fellowship with other Christians that will in turn encourage us and help equip us to share our faith with the lost world around us. We must not lose focus on this. If we do, we will complain more and fight with each other, and then the lost world around us will not want to be a part of us.

Now read Phil. 2:16.

What should we hold fast to?

I feel that I am just repeating myself by typing this, but I must. We need to be connected to God's word if we want to know how to obey Him and if we want to stay close to Him. My translation says *word of life*. We should see the Word of God as something that sustains us. Likewise, our churches need to be focused on teaching the word of God. Our culture tends to think that we need another big program or some flashy way to bring people into the church. But in reality, our churches need more of the Word of God (which brings life) being taught than anything else. Our churches need to be different from the world. Some churches think they have to compromise what the Bible says to get people in the doors. But when we compromise the word of God, we are not teaching people how to live their lives in obedience with God. They will miss out on God's peace and many blessings.

Why did Paul want for them to *hold fast to the word of life*?

Paul wanted to go to heaven and hear from God that the Christians he disciple followed after God. Paul wanted to know that all He was doing for Christ was not in vain. Paul wanted to know that he had done what God wanted him to do. He wanted these disciples to be the result of Paul's own life of obedience to God.

Think about it. How well does your church *hold fast* to the Word of God? Is your church different from the world?

Answer: if you help with a ministry in your church, how can you help make sure that that specific ministry holds fast to God's Word? End today by seeking God's answer to this question. Write your answer below.

Week Four, Day Two: A Sacrifice and a Drink Offering

Please begin with prayer.

On the space below, write out your Bible verse for this week. Then, spend at least five minutes analyzing the scripture. Refer to day one so you can remember what you need to be looking for.

_____

_____

_____

_____

_____

_____

_____

_____

_____

_____

_____

_____

_____

_____

_____

I know we have not been covering a lot of verses this week, and honestly, we will only look at two (in Philippians today), but I promise we will be covering larger passages of Philippians tomorrow, so please be patient with me!

Now read Phil. 2:17–18.

You might not really know what a drink offering is, so let me explain. A drink offering went along with a sacrifice. Every kind of offering or sacrifice listed had a drink offering that you poured out over the sacrifice. To put it in simple terms, the drink offering was seen as the second part of the sacrifice. In this passage, the sacrifice Paul is talking about is the sacrifice that the Philippians made for Paul. We already know that they sent Paul a gift to help him during his time he was in prison (and we will talk more about this tomorrow), but it is important to note that this gift they sent was not given out of the church's surplus of money. The church members sacrificed to be able to give this gift to Paul.

This was not the first time the Church of Philippi helped Paul. In 2 Corinthians, Paul thanks the churches of Macedonia (Philippi, Thessalonica, and Berea) for sending money to help the Christians in need in the Jerusalem church. Read 2 Corinthians 8:1–5.

According to 2 Cor. 8:3, did the church give right at what they could afford, or did they go beyond?

The Church of Philippi gave to help this cause not because they had an overabundance of extra money in their budget but because they sacrificed and then were able to give. Some time had gone by since the writing of the letter to the Church of Corinth (2 Corinthians) and the letter to the Church of Philippi (Philippians), but the Church of Philippi was still willing to give sacrificially to help others.

Now, back to our passage in Philippians. The gift that the Philippians sent to Paul was the sacrifice Paul was talking about. Paul said that he was the drink offering being poured out over their sacrifice. Some people think this means that Paul thought that he was about to die and that is why he referred to himself as a drink offering. But others hold that Paul was really saying that compared to their sacrificial giving, he was second. Let us look at how these verses fit in with this section.

Reread Phil. 2:12–18. Summarize what Paul had been talking about in verses 12–15.

Taking all of this into account, I think Paul is showing us how they were being obedient. They were proving that they were *children of God* and they were holding to the Word of God.

I know that they were holding to the Word of God because the act of living a life of sacrifice—to be able to give back to God—is something that God has been convicting my husband and I about recently. It all started when we did a study of the Sermon on the Mount with our youth group. So, if you will indulge with me, we are going to look at what Jesus says about money and giving in the Sermon on the Mount.

Go ahead and read Matthew 6:19–21.

Where should we store up our treasures?

Where should we *not* store up our treasures, and why?

Read Matthew 6:22–23. This part of the passage might seem a little confusing. The best way I can explain it is that if we focus our mind (or our eye) on God's desires, then we will want to obey God and we will want to store up treasures in heaven. But if we focus our mind on things of this earth, then we will only think and want things of this earth.

What are some things on this earth that people might focus on and want to make a treasure of?

When we focus our mind on these things, then our whole body will not be full of light but full of darkness. The sad thing is, though we might not look or feel like we are full of darkness, when we compare our life with our treasures of this earth to a life full of storing up treasures in heaven, the life of darkness (which we think looks like the light) will in no way even come close to looking like light to us.

Now, write down Matthew 6:24.

Read Matthew 6:25–34. How does reading this passage make you more willing to give sacrificially?

I have always worried about money, but after studying this passage and really meditating on it, God showed me that I had way more treasures on this earth than I thought.

What, or who, do you think are your own personal treasures on earth?

I realized that things like my iPad and my cell phone were treasures I have on this earth. I realized that if something had happened to them, I would have been very upset. God showed me that these things are all just possessions, and I don't need to freak out if something happens to one of my earthly possessions because God is going to take care of my basic needs. After we realized this, my husband and I started giving money to people in need. In the past, if we heard of a need, we would normally not help because we don't have that much money ourselves, and it did not fit into our *budget*. But now, if we hear of a need, we give! You know what? God still took care of us. We still have the money to buy food and to pay our bills, but my husband and I took it another step. Now we do have a strict budget, and we only have a small amount of money for things that we don't really need (ex. eat out money, toys, and extra things like unneeded new clothes or jewelry). We are trying to sacrifice some things so we in turn can give more money to God. When I read that the Church of Philippi was doing this, and I knew that they were doing this because they most likely had been taught what Jesus said about money, I had to share!

Write out the end of 2:17, and then all of 2:18.

Paul rejoiced over the way the Philippian Church was living out their faith by sacrificially giving. This brought him much joy, but he wanted to make sure that they shared this joy with him.

Are you willing to sacrifice some earthly pleasures or treasures to be able to store up more treasures in heaven? If so, what are you willing to sacrifice?

You will find joy in the sacrifice and you will be able to rejoice, and remember, don't worry because God will take care of you!

Week Four, Day Three: Timothy and Epahroditus

Please begin with prayer.

On the space below, write out your Bible verse for this week. Then, spend at least five minutes analyzing the scripture. Refer to day one so you can remember what you need to be looking for.

_____

_____

_____

_____

_____

_____

_____

_____

_____

_____

_____

_____

_____

_____

_____

_____

_____

Read Phil. 2:19–24.

Why did Paul want to send Timothy?

"For I have no one else of _____ _____ who will _____ be concerned for your welfare" (Phil. 2:20 NASB).

Paul did not know anyone to send who would *genuinely be concerned* for the spiritual state of the people in Philippi. Paul could have said this because he knew that the members in Philippi and Timothy knew each other. After all, Paul says in Phil. 2:22, "the Church of Philippi knew Timothy's worth." I think it goes beyond that. Paul knew that Timothy was a true servant, and Paul was also very close with Timothy.

According to verses 2:21, what character trait did Timothy show?

Sounds familiar? Where else in the book of Philippians does Paul tell the Church of Philippi to put the needs of others before themselves? (look back on week two, day five if you need help)

Timothy was an example of what Paul was teaching the Philippians, so he was a great person for Paul to send on his behalf. But sending Timothy was a sacrifice for Paul. How can we deduce this by looking at Phil. 2:23?

This was not the first time or the last time that Paul would sent Timothy to a church for him. Read the following passages and note where and why Paul sent Timothy.

1 Corinthians 1:2 and 4:14–17

1 Thess. 1:1 and 3:1–3

1 Timothy 1:4–9

Paul trusted Timothy. Paul had been pouring everything into Timothy, what he was teaching his churches, and Timothy was following everything he learned. Timothy was following Paul's example so much that Paul could write to the Church of Corinth, and say, "Therefore I exhort you, be imitators of me. For this reason, I have sent to you Timothy, who is my beloved and faithful child in the Lord, and he will remind you of my ways which are in Christ, just as I teach everywhere in every church." Just like the passage in Philippians, Paul referred to Timothy more than once as a *son*.

Timothy was Paul's disciple. Paul led many people to Christ, and then started churches so those people could be discipled. Timothy was one of the main disciples of Paul. It reminds me of Star Wars. I know that I am mainly writing this Bible study for ladies, so some of you might not get the Star Wars reference. In Star Wars, each Jedi master has an apprentice who follows them and learns how to be a Jedi master.

Once they have completed their training, they become Jedi masters and get their own apprentice, and the circle continues. I see Paul as the master, and Timothy as the apprentice. Our churches seem to be lacking relationships like what Paul and Timothy had. Adults don't seek out young people to disciple, and young people don't seek out adults to disciple them. If we really want the Gospel to spread, we need to be making more disciples and building relationships in our churches.

If you are young or you feel that you are not ready to have a disciple, who do you think God wants to be your mentor?

If you feel you are ready to have a disciple, who do you think God wants to be your disciple?

Yes, we are all disciples of Christ, but just going to church isn't cutting it. If we want to make a difference for Christ and we want to be like Him, then we will make disciples. After all, the Great Commission does not just tell us to *go*, but it also tells us to make disciples. We do not need to forget this part! Right now, I have three young ladies who I am teaching and trying to pour into. One of them is a new Christian. I will call her Ann. Her parents are Buddhists and do not know that she is a Christian. Today, I got a text from Ann while a group that I'm in from our church was helping set things up for a mission project. In the text, she told me that she had some family friends visiting and they had been in a really bad car accident. She asked us to pray for them. Right away, we all stopped and prayed. Then, we had to do more than that. Our pastor left to go to the hospital, and my husband and I (with a small group of people) went to

Ann's house. When we got there, we were talking with Ann's parents, and her dad looked at me, and said "You are AJ. You are the one who takes care of Ann!" I think that is the best compliment I have ever been given. Yet, I still feel like I don't do enough. But I am glad that her parents notice something is different about us, and I am praying that they will turn to God. Please don't think that I wrote that story to make you think that I am better than you. I know I am not. I wrote it to show you that we all need to be disciplining younger Christians.

Now read Phil. 2:25–30.

How is Epaphroditus described by Paul?

We know that Paul wrote this letter as a thank you note for the gift of support that the Church of Philippi sent him. Epaphroditus was the messenger who brought that gift to Paul. The plan was for Epaphroditus not only to bring the gift, but also to stay and help support Paul.

According to Phil. 2:26–27, what happened to Epaphroditus?

Epaphroditus most likely became sick on his journey to see Paul. He could have turned around and not completed the task given to him by his church, but he chose to continue on to see Paul. He wanted to give Paul the gift from the church. He had planned to stay and help Paul, but due to his sickness, he most likely was not able to be of any help to Paul. His sickness had gotten so bad that he almost died. Most likely, the Church of Philippi had heard about

Epaphroditus' condition and were concerned about him. Therefore, Paul was going to send him back to the church. It is believed that if Paul was sending him back that he must have been well enough to travel at this point.

Read Phil. 2:29–30. What did Paul ask the Philippians to do when Epaphroditus returned?

Epaphroditus did complete part of his mission by giving Paul the gift, but he was not able to complete the whole mission because the church also wanted him to physically stay there and help Paul. This did not upset Paul. Paul even reminded them that Epaphroditus risked "his life to complete what was deficient in your service to me." In other words, every single person who gave to help Paul in the Philippian Church could not make the journey to see Paul. They were *deficient*, but Epaphroditus was able to complete this mission.

This passage encourages me because it reminds me that our plans do not always work out, but we should not be upset by this. The church's plan was for Epaphroditus to stay with Paul, but that did not happen and Paul was okay with that. How many times do we get upset with a church member or a fellow Christian who has not completely carried out all of *our* plan? Maybe we should have the same attitude as Paul and be grateful for what was done and not stress over the part that did not get carried out. This might help our churches be better unified.

Is there a situation or person who did not complete a job or task in your church that has upset you? If so, end today by praying and asking God to help you forgive this person. Ask God to help you see that He is still in control even if things did not turn out the way you thought they should.

Week Four, Day Four: Beware of False Teachers

Start today with prayer. Pray that God will open your heart, speak to you, help you understand this scripture, show you how to apply these truths, and give you the power to apply His Word to your life.

On the space below, write out your Bible verse for this week. Then, spend at least five minutes analyzing the scripture. Refer to day one so you can remember what you need to be looking for.

_____

_____

_____

_____

_____

_____

_____

_____

_____

_____

_____

_____

_____

_____

_____

Today we are going to start chapter 3. I must say that this chapter has challenged me. After studying this chapter, I think I might now realize why there are not that many Bible studies on the book of Philippians! We are going to press on! I have prayed over what to write, and I think God has given me the words to best explain this chapter. So, buckle up and begin with prayer. This is going to be a fun ride!

Go ahead and read Phil. 3:1–3.

Paul starts off by telling them to do what in verse one?

Some scholars think that Paul is now starting to close his letter since he wrote *finally*, or that maybe there is a missing part to the letter and that is why he says this. I don't think either are the case. I think Paul was just transitioning into his next thought. I must say, I did not think much about this verse, but then when I was done studying all of chapter 3 and I sat down to start writing, I read this verse again and it jumped out at me! So, we are going to come back to this verse at the end of chapter 3.

What does Paul warn them to look out for? (Verse 2)

1.

2.

3.

This was not a list describing three separate groups, but it was three characteristics of one group of false teachers. The false teachers were Jews who were trying to convert the Christians in Philippi. The first description of them was that they were *dogs*. Eastern people most of the time did not like dogs. You could even say they hated dogs.

The Jews hated the Gentiles so much that they were referred to as dogs, but here, Paul flips it and he calls these Jews the dogs. Paul might have pictured these Jews like wild dogs roaming around searching for leftover food, but instead of looking for food, these Jews were following Paul and seeking out weak members from his churches to try and convert.

Next, Paul calls them *evil workers*. Jews believed that you could earn your salvation by following the law. It was their works that would get them into heaven. Lastly, Paul calls them the *false circumcision* (other translations might say *mutilators of the flesh;* even here, it is talking about a false circumcision). These Jews saw circumcision as the first step in following the law. Paul knew that this circumcision was only a physical cutting, and apart from Christ, it meant nothing.

Now, list how Paul describes the Christians in Philippi.

1.

2.

3.

4.

Paul is contrasting the Jewish false teachers with the Christians. Every true Christian should be able to see these in their own lives. First, the Christians are the true circumcision because they cut away sinful parts of their lives to follow Christ.

Col. 2:11 (NIV) says, "In him you were also circumcised with a circumcision not performed by human hands. Your whole self-ruled by the flesh was put off when you were circumcised by Christ."

What does this verse say about being circumcised?

Second, we are people who *worship in the Spirit of God*. To the Jews, worship was a tradition and a ritual. Something that was done to look good in front of others and God. We should not worship God out of ritual, but we should worship God because He deserves our worship. We should not go to worship so we can look good in front of others and because it is a ritual.

Next, it says that we *glory in Christ Jesus*, or other translations might say that we *boast in Christ Jesus*. The Jews boasted in what they had done—their works. But according to this passage, who should a true Christian boast or glory in?

You might not think that you have a problem with this one. Do you realize that you can't do anything on your own? God is the one who gives you breath each morning. He is the one who has given you everything you own, not you. We think that *we* do so much for ourselves, but in reality, we should not boast. We should look to Jesus

Christ and thank Him for giving us a job, a house, and our children. Everything comes from Him.

Lastly, true Christians *put no confidence in the flesh*. Jews believed that they could do good works to earn their way into heaven. They believed they had to follow the law, but true Christians know that we cannot do it on our own. The only way to heaven is through Jesus. We can never be good enough to make it into heaven without Jesus. I don't think too many Christians struggle with this one. I think that we all understand that we can't be good enough to get into heaven on our own. That is why we have asked Jesus to save us. I do think we can forget why we do the things that we do. I think that just like worship we can try to do good things to please others, but not really because we are doing them out of a serving heart for God. I think that this can lead us to believe that when we serve God, we have a higher standing with God. This makes us proud and makes us think that we are better than non-Christians and even some Christians. We can become arrogant.

Remember in week one, day two when the Jewish people killed Stephen. They really believed that what they were doing was right. As Christians, we often look at the Pharisees, Sadducees, and Jewish leaders of Jesus's time as the enemy. We need to realize that they were the church of their day. They were the people who were waiting on the Messiah to come. They just did not understand that Jesus was the Messiah because they were not really seeking and following God with a pure heart. Most of them believed that they could earn their way into heaven. They thought they had everything figured out, and they did not want for anything to change and they were arrogant. Friends, we might not be tempted to follow other religions but we will be tempted to be like the Pharisees, Sadducees, and the Jewish leaders.

So, I want you to look at the four things that we should be doing (in contrast to the ways the Jewish leaders were), and I want you to pray over each one and ask God if you struggle in any way with these. Write what God tells you below.

1. God, do I really have a circumcised heart free from old sins?

2. God, do I worship you like a true Christian? Is it just out of ritual that I worship you? Or do I worship you to just look good in front of others?

3. God, do I boast in you when good things happen? Or do I give myself the credit and forget about you?

4. God, do I find my confidence that I am going to heaven from Jesus Christ's redeeming action on the cross? Or do I sometimes think that I can do enough good deeds to get into heaven? Do I sometimes think that I am better than other Christians?

Do not feel bad. No Christian is perfect. We will struggle with these things from time to time. Although we might not have Jews trying to convert us in our churches today, we can still learn that we need to be diligent to make sure that we are following Christ. When we begin to struggle with anything from the above list, we need to seek out help from God and our fellow church members to hold us accountable.

To end on a positive note, write about the one area (of the four things from the list) where God has helped you improve the most!

Week Four, Day Five:
Week in Review

Today, I want you to begin with prayer (like all of the rest of the days). Pray that God will open your heart, speak to you, help you understand this scripture, show you how to apply these truths, and give you the power to apply His Word to your life. Make sure you pray for the requests that your group shared.

On the space below, write out your Bible verse for this week. Then, spend at least five minutes analyzing the scripture.

_____

_____

_____

_____

_____

_____

_____

_____

_____

_____

_____

_____

I want you to go back and reread Phil. 2:13–3:3 and Matthew 6:19–23. Then without looking back on your notes, try to summarize what you learned from these passages. What did you learn about God's character from these passages? Did God specifically tell you to do something this week? Write your review and answers down. After you do this, go back and flip through the week and make any extra notes of things you forgot but you want to make sure you don't forget next time you read these passages.

_____
_____
_____
_____
_____
_____
_____
_____
_____
_____
_____
_____
_____
_____
_____
_____
_____
_____
_____
_____
_____

Small Group Questions

1. Refer to your review day and take turns sharing with your group your summary of what happened in the Scriptures you read this week.

2. What did God specifically teach you this week? Did God tell you to do something specific this week? Did you learn something new about God's character? If you need to, refer to the review day and take turns sharing with the group.

3. Share with each other areas that you are struggling with that you need prayer. Do not be scared to open up and share. God wants us to lift each other up in prayer. Ask for prayer that God will help you with anything He has told you to do. Write down everyone's prayer requests, and commit to praying for your friends during the week when you do this study. End your time together by praying specifically for each request.

_____

_____

_____

_____

_____

_____

_____

_____

_____

_____

_____

_____

_____

_____

Week Four M and M Bible Verses

"Further, my brothers and sisters, rejoice in the Lord! It is no trouble for me to write the same things to you again, and it is a safeguard for you" (Phil. 3:1).

"What is more, I consider everything a loss because of the surpassing worth of knowing Christ Jesus my Lord, for whose sake I have lost all things. I consider them garbage, that I may gain Christ" (Phil. 3:8).

"Brothers and sisters, I do not consider myself yet to have taken hold of it. But one thing I do: Forgetting what is behind and straining toward what is ahead" (Phil. 3:13).

"I press on toward the goal to win the prize for which God has called me heavenward in Christ Jesus" (Phil. 3:14).

"But our citizenship is in heaven. And we eagerly await a Savior from there, the Lord Jesus Christ" (Phil. 3:20).

Week Five, Day One:
Confidence in the Flesh

Please begin with prayer.

On the space below, write out your Bible verse for this week. Then, spend at least five minutes analyzing the scripture. Refer to day one so you can remember what you need to be looking for.

_____

_____

_____

_____

_____

_____

_____

_____

_____

_____

_____

_____

_____

_____

_____

_____

By studying this letter to the Church of Philippi, I have realized that I personally need to change many things in my life. I already talked about that when dealing with church unity. I have at times thought that I knew the Bible better than other church members. I had an attitude of "I am right and they are wrong!" I think this comes from my background. You see, I grew up in a Christian home. I am one of those people who can say that they were going to church even while they were still in their mother's womb. My mother even worked on staff at our church, but I can go beyond that. I also graduated from a Christian high school, and then went on to a private Christian college where I majored in Christian Studies. I graduated with a BA in Christian Studies, and then I even went on to marry a minister. I have always seen these things as great things in my life, and although I still believe that all of these things are good things, God has started to show me that I have become arrogant. I believed that I was better than other Christians because of all of these opportunities I had. God has shown me that I have been very wrong. I am no better than other Christians.

Read Phil. 3:4–6.

List the seven things Paul says gave him confidence in his flesh.

1.

2.

3.

4.

5.

6.

7.

The first four were qualifications Paul got from his family, and the last three were ones that Paul achieved on his own. The Jews loved groups that strictly followed the law, and one of those groups was the Pharisees. Paul was a Pharisee. In the first century, Jews thought that you had an extra level of commitment if you were willing to persecute people who followed a different religion. Paul had taken this extra step of *zeal*. The Jews also believed that you could follow the law close enough and do enough *good* to earn the level of being *blameless*. Paul had also done this. If these Jews who were trying to convert the new Christians had been able to read this letter, then they would have been very impressed by Paul's past. After looking at Paul's list, these Jews would have thought that Paul had enough works on his list to get him into heaven.

Next, Paul is going to show the Christians in the church that although he was once like those Jews, he has changed. Read Phil. 3:7–9.

According to verse 7, what did Paul see as a *loss*?

Fill in the blanks for verse 8.

"More than that, I count ____things to be _____ in _____ of knowing Christ Jesus my Lord" (NASB).

According to verses 8 and 9, what did Paul gain because of his *loss?*

How many times does Paul say *loss* in this passage?

What did Paul call all these things he had lost compared to Christ? (Verse 8)

Compared to knowing Christ and having a relationship with Him, all of those other things were a loss! We can grow up in Christian homes, go to church every time the doors are open, go to school, get a degree in Christian studies, and volunteer to help others in the name of Christ. But all of those things are *nothing* compared to *knowing* Christ and having a personal relationship with Him! God has shown me that my past is a good thing, but all of these *good works* do not compare to my relationship with Christ. It is better for me to know him personally than to just look good in front of others.

According to verse 9, Paul did not want his righteousness to come from what? What did Paul want to find his righteousness in?

Paul realized that being *blameless* was not going to get him into heaven. The law was meant to show the Jews that they could never be good enough to earn their salvation. The law was not the problem, but sin was the problem. Even the best person in the world cannot come close to earning their salvation.

After reading about the good works that Paul found confidence in and hearing my own story, I want you to end today by looking at your own past and writing down anything that you have/can be tempted to put your confidence in other than Christ.

<u>Things from Your Family</u>   <u>Things You Earned</u>

After writing your list, pray and ask God to forgive you if you have put confidence in any of these things. If there is anything on the list that you might be tempted to put your confidence in, ask God to help you be so close to Him that you would never put confidence in other things ever again.

Week Five, Day Two:
Sanctification

Please begin today with prayer, and then read Phil. 3:10–11.

On the space below, write out your Bible verse for this week. Then, spend at least five minutes analyzing the scripture. Refer to day one so you can remember what you need to be looking for.

_____

_____

_____

_____

_____

_____

_____

_____

_____

_____

_____

_____

_____

_____

_____

_____

_____

_____

First, let us look at the term *resurrection power*, or other translations might say *the power of his resurrection*. Not only did this power raise Christ from the dead, but also now lives in true Christians and gives us the power to have a new life in Christ.

How are you encouraged to know that you have the same power that raised Christ from the dead living inside of you?

After realizing this, how do you think this will change your outlook on life?

Next, let us look at *fellowship of His suffering*. Paul wanted to know Christ more and be able to identify with Christ. Paul wanted to suffer for Christ so he could change and be more like Christ. Just like Paul, we need to choose every day to die to our sinful and selfish desires. We need to choose to deny ourselves and pick up our cross and follow Christ every day.

Last, let us look at "being conformed to His death; in order that I may attain to the resurrection from the dead." When I started studying this phrase, I came across the term *sanctification*. I had heard this term in college, but I did not remember what it meant. As I started studying this term, I started to love it more and more. Before I can talk about sanctification, we need to talk about another term which is *justification*.

Justification is when we are made justified in the eyes of God. If you go back and read Phil. 3:9, we see that our righteousness comes from our faith in Christ, not in our works. This word used for righteousness is a legal term used in court. So when one of the false

Jewish teachers stood before God in judgment and God asked what they had done to deserve to get into heaven, they would say they had kept the law, but that was not enough. When a Christian stands in front of God on the day of judgment, they can say that they are righteous because of Jesus's blood. When a person becomes a Christian and chooses to make Jesus their Lord and Savior, they are justified. Justification happens when we are saved. It is a one-time thing *but* then comes sanctification.

Sanctification is a process where God and man work together throughout a Christian's life to make that person more and more like Christ, and God frees that Christian from the bondage of more and more sins. Christians should long to become more and more like Christ. We should long to be set free from our sins.

Now, let us go back to my story. I don't think that I pushed on people the option that I was better than them, but I am sure that friends have felt this about me. I think that most of the time, this feeling was deep in my heart but I tried not to show it. Even if I tried to hide this feeling, that does not mean I wasn't wrong. God wanted to change *all* of me. He wants to set me free from all of my sins. Even the deep, dark parts that no one sees. Growing in Christ is a process, and we should all be looking for ways that we can become more and more like Him.

Stop right now and pray, ask God to reveal to you any deep dark sins that you have in your heart that others might not know about. Once God shows you this sin, ask God to help you be sanctified by helping you be free from the bondage of that sin! If you feel comfortable, write about that sin below.

Read Phil. 3:12.

True or False: According to verse 12, Paul realized that he already knew everything and was perfect.

Isn't it nice to realize that Paul of all people did not think that he was perfect? I find comfort in his humbleness, and it reminds me that no matter how close to God I get, I always need to remember that I am still not perfect.

Paul looked forward to the day he would be resurrected to heaven. He knew that this process of sanctification would only be complete when he got to heaven. Just like Paul, we will never be completely free from our sins while we are on this earth. But once we get to heaven, we will complete the sanctification process by being completely free from all sin!

Read Phil. 3:13–14, what did Paul say he forgot?

What was Paul reaching for?

Is there anything in your past that you need to forget so you can then look forward to what God has ahead for you? Write about it below.

In verses 13 and 14, Paul is using athletic images again. His readers would have noticed these terms because they were very familiar with the Greek athletic games. I am not a runner, but I do know that runners are put under both mental and physical strain so they have to be dedicated to race (if they want to reach their goal). I also read that runners are trained to focus their eyes on a certain spot when racing. Just like runners need to focus their eyes, we also need to focus our eyes on Christ if we want to reach our goal.

What are things in our lives that we can be tempted to focus our eyes on other than Christ?

What do you personally struggle with in focusing your eyes on other than Christ?

Remember that we are talking about sanctification here. Paul started his race at conversion (when he was justified), and he did not want to slow down. Paul wanted to reach his goal. He wanted to become more and more like Christ until he ultimately went to heaven. As Christians, we should not be satisfied just going to church once or twice a week and not living for Christ the rest of the week.

Remember that it is not enough to just study the Bible. We need to apply it to our lives. When our eyes are focused on other things, then we will not want to apply God's truths to our own lives. We must focus our eyes on Christ if we want to be able to become more and more like Him.

Now read 3:15–16. There is debate on who Paul is talking to when he says "as many as are perfect." Some believe Paul is talking to mature Christians who are like Paul. Others believe he could be talking to people who think they already know everything so they feel that they are *perfect* or *mature*. I personally think it is the second of the two because if they really are *perfect* or *mature* like Paul, then they would most likely already have this attitude.

Go back and read Phil. 3:12–14, and summarize the attitude that Paul had in these verses.

Once again, Paul is calling the church to unity by telling them to realize that they are not perfect, and that everyone needs to be striving to forget the past and always strive to grow more and more in their walk with Christ. They should never think that they are complete and that they have nothing else to learn.

According to Phil. 3:15, who will reveal to people that they have the wrong attitude/thinking?

I think that as Christians, when someone has a bad attitude, we think that *we* need to be the ones to correct them. God does call Christians to hold each other accountable and to confront other Christians when they are living a life of sin, but before we confront people, we should first pray and ask God to reveal this wrong attitude to them! If they are Christians and they have the Holy Spirit living inside of them, He can talk to them and change them without us even talking to them.

Do you think if we first prayed for God to reveal things to other Christians before we confronted them that this would help with church unity?

Do you have confidence that God can change people? Write down an example of a time God changed your mind, or an example of when He changed another Christian's mind.

We cannot change people; only God can. We can help the process by praying for God to change them. Pray that God will open their hearts and minds so they can hear God speak to them. You have been praying that God will speak to you and teach you, then why not pray for others as well? It isn't going to hurt. If anything, it might even help in the way that you view that person. After all, it is hard to be mad at someone you are praying for!

Is there a friend in your church that you believe has the wrong attitude or thinking? End today by praying and asking God to change their hearts, then ask God to reveal to you if you have any wrong attitudes or wrong thoughts in your heart as well.

Week Five, Day Three: Paul's Example

Please begin with prayer.

On the space below, write out your Bible verse for this week. Then, spend at least five minutes analyzing the scripture. Refer to day one so you can remember what you need to be looking for.

_____
_____
_____
_____
_____
_____
_____
_____
_____
_____
_____
_____
_____
_____
_____
_____
_____

As Christians, we often have people looking at us to be a good example of who Christ is. This might scare some people, and this might be the reason why some people do not want to disciple other believers because they do not want to have that much pressure put on them, but Paul welcomed this challenge!

Read Phil. 3:17.

Whose example did Paul want for them to follow?

Paul wanted the Christians to look to him (and other believers) as an example of Christ. Don't think that Paul was being arrogant when he said this. Back then, Christians did not have the New Testament, so the best way for them to learn how to be like Jesus was to follow the example of other more mature Christians. Paul had already told them to be like Christ in chapter 2. When Paul asked them to follow his example, he was doing so because he knew by following him they would in turn be following Christ.

Are you close enough to Christ that you can tell others to follow your example?

Read Phil. 3:18–19.

According to verse 18, what was Paul doing when he wrote about these people who are enemies of the cross?

This is the only time that Paul talks about crying while he is writing a letter. Paul could have cried when he wrote other letters, but this is the only time Paul felt the need to tell his readers that he was crying. Take a break to just pause and think about the fact that Paul cried over the fact that these Jews were lost and their way led to destruction. He most likely was talking about the same Jewish teachers who were trying to lead these Christians away from faith in Christ. He was not mad at them. He was crying over their salvation.

How does Paul describe this group in verse 19?

Their end is their destruction because these Jews believed that they were on their way to heaven by trying to fulfill the law. They cared more about how they ate and what they ate than the state of their heart. They felt they gained glory from God by living a life according to the law, but, really, it only made them arrogant. In the end, because their minds were more on how to fulfill the law, they were focused more on earthly things than heavenly things, and this made Paul very sad.

Remember to week one, day two, was Paul alone on the road to Damascus? (Read Acts 9:7)

Paul was not alone, and we do not know what happened to these people who were with him. Even if those friends with him did get saved, Paul still would have had many other friends who were still Jews. Because Paul was willing to persecute the Christians and had so much zeal, he might have been friends with these same Jews who were now trying to convert his own Christian friends. I am sure that he tried to witness to these Jews, but they did not want to believe. This made Paul very sad. Why did Paul tell the Church of Philippi that he cared so much about these Jews that he cried over them being lost?

What had Paul just told them to do in verse 3:17?

I think Paul wanted them to share his sadness and realize that we should all be sad when anyone around us is lost, even if it is people who persecute us or try to lead us astray. These people need Christ, too. We are often tempted to get mad at people who treat us badly, or look down on people who live lives full of sin. But do you ever stop to look at people the way God does? God is sad. We should be sad that they do not know God.

Read Phil. 3:20–21.

Where is our citizenship?

The people in Philippi would have had a strong connection with Paul talking about their citizenship. They were all Roman citizens. Part of being a Roman citizen meant that they had to wait to hear from Rome on different laws. As Christians, they were waiting on their Savior Jesus.

What is going to happen when Jesus returns? (Verse 21)

Once again, Paul is talking about sanctification. I know I look forward to when Christ returns. What do you look forward to the most about the day your humble body is transformed?

Now that we are done with chapter 3, I want you to go back and read Philippians 3:1. Paul says that "rejoicing in the Lord is a safeguard or protection for us." At the end of Philippians 3, we see that God has the power to "bring all things into subjection to himself." Hard times will come. We will be tempted to follow the wrong path or the wrong way of thinking, but we need to always focus on Christ and rejoice in Him. I believe Paul started chapter 3 like this because he knew that by focusing on Christ, they would then have a safeguard from the temptation to not follow Christ.

Do you think that if you rejoiced more in the Lord and focused more on heaven in your everyday life that you would be less likely to be tempted?

Therefore, let us *rejoice* over this! As we wait for Jesus's return, let us rejoice over the fact that God has this power to change our lives and will not stop until we get to heaven!

Week Five, Day Four:
Live in Harmony

Please begin today with prayer.

On the space below, write out your Bible verse for this week. Then, spend at least five minutes analyzing the scripture. Refer to day one so you can remember what you need to be looking for.

_____

_____

_____

_____

_____

_____

_____

_____

_____

_____

_____

_____

_____

_____

_____

_____

_____

_____

Start off by reading Phil. 4:1.

What two things did Paul call them?

How many times does Paul call them his beloved in verses 1–3?

Once again, Paul is showing how much he really cared for this group of Christians because he said that he longed to see them, and he called them his beloved two times in one sentence (other translations say *dear friends* and *my brothers*)! I do not believe that Paul's joy came from his fellow Christians. Paul's joy came from God, but he found extra joy in knowing these Christians. God brought me joy through one of our youth this week, and I wanted to share the story.

Our house is for sale for right now. I got a call earlier this week that a cash buyer wanted to come see our house that same day in a few hours, and if you have sold a house within the past few years in this *buyers' market*, you jump at anyone looking at your house. So I started cleaning, and then I remembered that the grass needed to be mowed. I then asked my husband if he thought it would be a good idea to ask one of our youth (who has a business mowing yards) if he could come over and mow the yard before the people came to look at the house. My husband said he would talk to him. About an hour later, I heard a mower in the backyard. I looked, and there he was. I was very grateful that he made time for us. I then started to think about the great group of young people we have in our church, and how very proud I am of them because I do see Jesus in them. Then later when we saw him at church and I told him I needed to pay him, he responded with "No, you don't need to pay me anything!" I found much joy in this. Not because I did not have to pay him, but because I knew he was doing this as an act of kindness to us. I had joy because I was proud that he cared more about us than making money.

I think this is the same type of joy that Paul felt. Paul had taught these Christians, and he found joy when he heard about them following Christ. This type of joy comes from pouring your life into another person and watching them grow in Christ.

Do you have anyone in your life who you have taught and later found joy in like this? If so, write about the person and the situation below.

If you cannot think of anyone, that is okay, but I do encourage you to invest in the lives of the Christians around you. Yes, your joy needs to come from Christ, but you can find extra joy in serving and disciplining other Christians.

Because Paul called them his *own*, this would have made the Philippians think of heaven. Remember, Paul was just talking about heaven in Philippians 3:20–21, so it is not odd that he references something about them being his crown shortly after.

Paul told them to do something in verse 4:1 that he has already told them before, what is it?

Paul said this first in Philippians 1:27, and now in Philippians 4:1, he says, "In this way stand firm." What *way* is Paul talking about? Let us look at everything Paul said between the first *stand firm* and the second *stand firm*. Paul told them to have an *untied mind*. To be like Christ by putting other people's needs before their own. To live our lives in obedience to God. To not be like the false teachers who put their hope in things of this earth, and who believed they could earn their own salvation and to keep our eyes on our goal which is to be more and more like Christ every day until we make it to heaven. That is a lot! These are all things that we need to be doing to make sure we are standing firm in the Lord.

Read Phil. 4:2–3.

You can tell that Paul felt strongly about them coming into harmony and being able to work this out because he urged both of them to work it out. Somehow, the church had found out about this disagreement and sent word to Paul about it because they were not able to solve this on their own. They wanted Paul's opinion on the matter, but something is missing in this letter about the situation.

Did you notice what is missing? If so, write it below.

Paul did not address the specific issue that these two women were fighting over. This tells us that the issue was not something that Paul felt he needed to address. Therefore, it was not something that the Bible clearly says is wrong or right. They could have been fighting over who was going to be in charge of a certain ministry, or maybe one felt like they were doing too much church work and the other woman was not doing enough work, or it could have just been a personality difference the women had with each other. I am just guessing. We do not know what the issue was.

Paul did not tell them who was right or wrong, but he did say something he wanted both of them to do. What did Paul tell them to do?

Paul did not just tell them to get along or to get over it. He told them to *live in harmony in the Lord*, or some translations say to *be of the same mind in the Lord*. In my mind, this means that they needed to turn to the Lord to find harmony with each other. This was not to be a one-time thing but a way that they should live! Paul wanted them to resolve this conflict on their own by turning to the Lord. Even if they still could not work it out, Paul called someone to help them. Paul called this person a *true companion* or *true partner*. This most likely was another church member.

What had these women shared with Paul?

Paul then goes on to remind them of how they shared struggles together as they shared the Gospel with others. He even reminds them of a fellow friend named Clement who worked with all of them. All of these people had their names written in the Book of Life. They were all Christians. They were all going to heaven, and were all family!

Can you think of any little issues that have upset you in your church that were not theological issues? Write about them below.

If this issue is still going on, Paul would like to urge you to *live in harmony* with these other people. Remember that this is your heavenly family. We should love our family and be willing to forgive them. We should also humbly put their interest before our own.

Read what Jesus said in Matthew 5:21–23.

According to Jesus, what is the same thing as murdering someone?

Jesus tells them to leave the altar if they realize what?

Do you need to do this with anyone in your church? Pray and ask God.

Jesus and Paul both want Christians to work out their differences. We need to realize that we are all family. We should be more like Jesus and be willing to forgive and put the needs of others before our own. Then, our church will see even more unity.

Week Five, Day Five:
Week in Review

Today, I want you to begin with prayer (like all of the rest of the days). Pray that God will open your heart, speak to you, help you understand this scripture, show you how to apply these truths, and give you the power to apply His Word to your life. Make sure you pray for the requests that your group shared.

On the space below, write out your Bible verse for this week. Then, spend at least five minutes analyzing the scripture.

_____

_____

_____

_____

_____

_____

_____

_____

_____

_____

_____

_____

I want you to go back and reread Phil. 3:4–4:3 and Matthew 5:21–24. Then without looking back on your notes, try to summarize what you learned from these passages. What did you learn about God's character from these passages? Did God specifically tell you to do something this week? Write your review and answers down. After you do this, go back and flip through the week and make any extra notes of things you forgot but you want to make sure you don't forget next time you read these passages.

_____
_____
_____
_____
_____
_____
_____
_____
_____
_____
_____
_____
_____
_____
_____
_____
_____
_____
_____
_____
_____
_____
_____

Small Group Questions

1. Refer to your review day and take turns sharing with your group your summary of what happened in the Scriptures you read this week.

2. What did God specifically teach you this week? Did God tell you to do something specific this week? Did you learn something new about God's character? If you need to, refer to the review day and take turns sharing with the group.

3. Share with each other areas that you are struggling with that you need prayer. Do not be scared to open up and share. God wants us to lift each other up in prayer. Ask for prayer that God will help you with anything He has told you to do. Write down everyone's prayer requests, and commit to praying for your friends during the week when you do this study. End your time together by praying specifically for each request.

_____
_____
_____
_____
_____
_____
_____
_____
_____
_____
_____
_____
_____
_____
_____
_____

Week Five M and M Bible Verses

"Rejoice in the Lord always. I will say it again: Rejoice! 5 Let your gentleness be evident to all. The Lord is near" (Phil. 4:4–5).

"Do not be anxious about anything, but in every situation, by prayer and petition, with thanksgiving, present your requests to God. And the peace of God, which transcends all understanding, will guard your hearts and your minds in Christ Jesus" (Phil. 4:6–7).

"Finally, brothers and sisters, whatever is true, whatever is noble, whatever is right, whatever is pure, whatever is lovely, whatever is admirable—if anything is excellent or praiseworthy—think about such things" (Phil. 4:8).

"I know what it is to be in need, and I know what it is to have plenty. I have learned the secret of being content in any and every situation, whether well fed or hungry, whether living in plenty or in want. I can do all this through him who gives me strength" (Phil. 4:12–13).

"The grace of the Lord Jesus Christ be with your spirit. Amen" (Phil. 4:23).

Week Six, Day One:
Rejoice in the Lord!

Start today with prayer. Pray that God will open your heart, speak to you, help you understand this scripture, show you how to apply these truths, and give you the power to apply His Word to your life.

On the space below, write out your Bible verse for this week. Then, spend at least five minutes analyzing the scripture. Refer to day one so you can remember what you need to be looking for.

_____

_____

_____

_____

_____

_____

_____

_____

_____

_____

_____

_____

_____

_____

I have two young children, and I often have to repeat myself with them. Sometimes I repeat myself before they even have the chance to be disobedient. The conversation might go something like this: "We are going out to eat and I want for the two of you to use your inside voices. You can play with your toys or color on the papers they give you, but I want for you to make sure that you use your inside voices. So, no yelling. I will say it one more time. Please use your inside voices." As adults, sometimes God has to repeat Himself several times to help us understand. Paul understood this, and repeated a lot of the same things in his letter to the Philippians.

Now that we have completed four weeks, what topics do you remember that Paul repeated in this letter?

Now read Philippian 4:4.

What did Paul tell them to do more than once?

Who are we to rejoice in?

This is the only time in his letter that he repeats himself right after he just said the same thing! So you know that it must be very important to rejoice, but not just simply rejoice. Paul says to *rejoice in the Lord*. But why didn't Paul just say to *rejoice* twice? There must be a difference between just rejoicing and rejoicing in the Lord. I think we see the difference in Kay Warren's definition of joy. She defines joy as "the settled assurance that God is in control of all the details of my life, the quiet confidence that ultimately everything is going to be all right, and the determined choice to praise God in all things." To *rejoice in the Lord* is to realize that He is in control, and that turning your life over to Him every day is the best way to find joy. Then, you will be able to *rejoice in the Lord*.

Read Jeremiah 29:11. What kind of plans does God have for you?

A lot of times people read this verse and think that it means that no bad things will ever happen to them, but it is important to know the context behind this verse. When Jeremiah told this to Israel, they were in the process of being taken over by Babylon. When God told Jeremiah this, He was telling the people that even if God let these things happen to them (that were bad), ultimately, this was a part of God's plan and He would bring something good out of their situation.

Do you believe that "God is in control of all the details of your life?" Do you believe that "ultimately, everything is going to be alright," even when bad things happen to you?

When is it hard for you to believe this? If you have a specific example, write about it below.

Read Phil.4:5. What kind of spirit does Paul want for them to have?

Who does Paul say should notice this spirit?

When I read this, I thought that a gentle spirit (other translations might say *graciousness*) was just a nice spirit. But when I started studying this passage, I found out that it was much deeper than that. The word for gentle here meant that they should have "the willingness to yield one's personal right and to show consideration and gentleness to others." Once again, Paul is telling them to think of other people's needs before their own needs. Paul wants all men to see this gentle spirit. That means your family members, your coworkers, members of your church, Christians outside of your church, non-Christians, and strangers who you don't even know if they are Christians or not! The more I study this book of the Bible and I see the many treasures on church unity, I started to think that our lives would have much more peace if we applied these principles to every area of our lives where we need unity. What if we applied them with our failing marriage? What if we applied them with our sibling who no longer talks to you? What if we applied them to our boss who makes our job miserable? We could include *everyone* in what we are learning about unity.

What area of your life do you want more unity (outside of your church)? Are you willing to apply these principles?

How well do you put the needs of *everyone* in your life before yourself?

I must admit that this is a hard concept to grasp. We often do not think to look for ways to love non-Christians or strangers around us. We do not think about this when we lose our patience in the checkout line at the grocery store because the line is so long or when we lose our temper with the young waitress that got our order wrong. No, we want good customer service and we want to be treated fairly. We do not take the time to stop and be gentle or show grace to the people around us. We might even think that we can't love *that* many people more than ourselves! Let us look at the next sentence. Paul tells them that "The Lord is near." Here, Paul isn't just saying that the Lord is all around and sees everything we do. This is true, but Paul is also saying that the Lord is near. As in, He will be coming back soon.

Read Matthew 24:36–44, and summarize.

This is why we should try to love everyone, and I mean, *everyone*. We love the waitress who got our order wrong. We love our boss who only yells at us. We love the cashier who has only heard people complain to her all day over how long her line has been. We love them so we can share the Gospel with the ones who are not saved. We also love our families and other church members so we can help them grow closer to Christ. Why? Because the Lord is near.

Do you have a lost friend or family member who you need to show a gentle spirit to? If so, write their name below. Pray and ask God to show you how to do this.

End today by praying, and ask God to give you the strength to find your joy in Him, and that you will be able to share His joy with *all* of the people that are around you.

Week Six, Day Two:
The Cure for Anxiety

Please begin today with prayer.

On the space below, write out your Bible verse for this week. Then, spend at least five minutes analyzing the scripture. Refer to day one so you can remember what you need to be looking for.

_____

_____

_____

_____

_____

_____

_____

_____

_____

_____

_____

_____

_____

_____

_____

_____

Today, we will be studying one of my all-time favorite scripture passages! It is one of my favorite because, since I can remember, I have always had a problem with anxiety. It got so bad last year that I even had to go to a therapist for help. Through the whole situation, God helped me to come out stronger, and I have never in my life had as much peace as I do right now.

Read Philippians 4:6–7.

If you are a worrier like me, you might find it hard to read a verse like Phil. 4:6. What does Paul say not to do?

According to Paul, what three things should we do instead of worrying?

We take that same power we use to worry, and instead, turn it into something good by praying. Paul tells them to do three things: pray, pray with supplication, and pray with thanksgiving. Paul made these into a list because they are three different ways to pray. The first one is to approach God in a state of worship realizing who He is. The second means to tell God what you need, and the third means that you remember that God has a perfect plan for your life even if bad things might happen. Remember that God is in control, and be thankful that your life is in His hands!

What will we get as a result of praying this way? (Verse 7)

What three things will the peace of God do?

"Transcends/surpasses all understanding" means that this peace from God will work better than any knowledge you might have. So even if you go to Bible study and after Bible study gain a lot of knowledge, unless you are willing to pray and ask God to help you when you are anxious, then that knowledge is not going to work that well. When we pray this way, the peace of God is then going to help us by guarding our hearts and our minds! The word *guard* here is a military term. So when you pray and ask God for His peace, He will send His military to guard both your mind and heart.

Paul separated these two, so what is the difference between our minds and our hearts? List the differences you can think of below.

Our hearts carry our emotions like love and fear. Our minds carry our thoughts like worry and anxiety. We need both to be protected if we want to truly have peace.

Now, let us practice this way of praying. Think of something that is going on in your life right now that you are worried or anxious about. Now write out your prayer by each step (I will list them below).

Step One: Pray approaching God in a state of worship. Praise Him for who He is.

Step Two: Tell God want you need and what is going on.

Step Three: Remember a time when God has taken care of you or brought you out of a hard situation like this. Remember that God has a perfect plan for your life, even if bad things might happen. Remember that God is in control, and be thankful that your life is in His hands. Thank Him for all of these things.

Read Philippians 4:8. Paul lists six things we should dwell on. When Paul is talking about *dwelling*, he is talking about the way we should think. Here is the list:

True—is a characteristic of God, so we are to think on things that are *valid, reliable,* and *honest.* We should think the way God thinks.

Noble—this word is mostly used to describe how church leaders should act, so we should think like a person who is respected and honorable.

Right—this means things that are *just* in view of God's standards, so we are not to think with earthly standards or act how the world says we should act. We should look at God's standards and what He says is *just* living and think on these things.

Pure—We should think on things that will make us morally pure in the eyes of God.

Lovely—We should think thoughts that make us pleasing to the people around us. Don't think a thought if you would not want someone to read your mind and know that thought.

Admirable—We should think on things that are *praiseworthy*, and we should seek not to offend people with our thoughts.

Paul lists these six things, and then he changes the sentence, and says, "If there is any excellence and if anything worthy of praise, dwell on these things." After Paul's long list, he sums everything up by telling his readers to "discern for themselves what is excellent and worthy of praise and dwell on these."

What does the word *dwell* mean? When Paul tells them to *dwell* on these things, he does not mean that you only think about these things one time or every now and then. Paul is saying that we should always dwell on these types of thoughts.

Think and list thoughts that we could have that are the opposite of the list above.

Which thoughts out of the top six do you struggle with the most?

Kay Warren reminded her readers in her book *Choose Joy* that, as Christians, if we want our emotions to change we need to be willing to change our thoughts first. Therefore, if you are mad at someone, instead of thinking negative thoughts about that person and just waiting for your anger to go away, change your thoughts and then you will find that your anger will go away much faster. I think that Paul realized that our thoughts are connected with our anxiety. Not only did Paul tell us *what to do* (pray with respect, tell God our needs, and be thankful that He is in control), he also told us *what not to do* by telling us to set our thoughts on more excellent and praiseworthy things.

Think of at least one situation where you may be tempted to think bad thoughts but you chose to think the right thoughts. Write about the situation, the bad thoughts you would be tempted to think, and the good thoughts you choose to think.

Do you spend more of your time thinking the thoughts from the bad list that you made or thoughts from Paul's list? Mark on this percentage line dividing your good thoughts and your bad thoughts. Then, write which side belongs to which.

10%   20%   30%   40%   50%   60%   70%   80%   90%   100%

I will be honest and say that I cannot mark that I have 100% good thoughts all the time. None of us are perfect. We will think *bad* thoughts, but we should not stay that way. When we realize we are thinking bad thoughts, we should ask forgiveness (and not wallow in guilt), and go right back to thinking the good thoughts again. Please let this exercise reveal how much you need to give God your thought life. Don't be disappointed by this exercise. Instead, be excited that God is going to help you do better!

Now read Phil. 4:9, how does Paul repeat himself again (look back at 3:17)? What is different this time?

Paul tells them to imitate him. But this time, he tells them to imitate him in what they learned from him, received from him, heard from him, and saw in him. If they did all this, they would have peace with God. Not only do we gain peace by praying and having the right thoughts, but we also gain peace by living out every part of our lives (what we teach people, how we help people, what we say to people, and how we act around people) in complete obedience to God. If you have been praying and you have the right thoughts yet you still do not have peace, ask God to search you and point out any area of disobedience you might have in your life that is blocking your peace.

Before we end today, I want to say that I have always loved studying this scripture. And this time, God showed me something that I had never realized before. This passage comes right after Paul had talked about the two women who had some kind of disagreement and could not get along. I believe that not only should we apply this passage to our own personal lives but that we should apply it to how we handle issues of disunity in our churches.

Look back over Phil. 4:6–9, and then write down how you think these principles could help with church unity.

I wish I could read your answers! God has slowly been giving me a heart for church unity. I believe that after studying today's lesson that when troubles or disagreements come up in our churches that we should stop and pray. Pray to the God that holds not just our lives in His hands, but also holds our churches. Tell God the needs that your church has. Thank God for all He has done for your church and realize that He has a plan. When we think about these issues of disunity, we should have our thoughts match up with the thoughts that Paul says. Lastly, we need to make sure that our churches are not being disobedient to God in some way. If individual Christians can disobey God, a church, as a whole, can as well. I hope this view of this passage will help you cultivate unity in your church, and I pray that God will give more Christians a heart for seeking unity in our churches.

Week Six, Day Three: The Secret to Being Content in All Things

Please begin today with prayer.

On the space below, write out your Bible verse for this week. Then, spend at least five minutes analyzing the scripture. Refer back to day one so you can remember what you need to be looking for.

_____

_____

_____

_____

_____

_____

_____

_____

_____

_____

_____

_____

_____

Yesterday, we studied one of my favorite passages in the Bible, Philippians 4:6–7. If that was not one of your favorites, then today, we will most likely be talking about one of your favorite Bible verses. Today we will be studying Philippians 4:10–14, which means Phil. 4:13 will be studied today!

Go ahead and read Phil. 4:10–14.

Paul begins by saying that he rejoiced over their renewed concern for him. We have already talked about how the Church of Philippi had a great love for Paul, and that they tried to help him as he spread the Gospel. But if Paul had already praised them for their support, why is he now saying that they have renewed their concern for him as if the church at some point had stopped supporting him?

The end of Phil. 4:10 gives us the reason why they stopped supporting Paul, what is the reason?

Some people might read this and think that they lacked the money or means to support Paul, but I do not believe that is the case. Since we have already studied how they sacrificed so they could help support Paul, I do not believe that they would have stopped because they did not have the means. They would have found a way. No, I (and other scholars) believe that they lacked opportunity because of where Paul was located, or maybe they were not able to contact Paul. Maybe while Paul was in jail in the beginning, he was not able to receive contact from his churches. Maybe the Church of Philippi had to search to find out where Paul was. I don't know exactly why they lacked opportunity.

According to Phil. 4:11, what had Paul learned?

Ah, contentment. I think it is safe to say that we all long for contentment. For a while now, I have believed that no matter what age you are you can/will always be looking forward to something (and you are not content until you get to the next stage in life). The child longs to be a teenager when they can stay up later and eat whatever they want to. The teenager long for the day they can drive, and then one day go to college or just simply get out of their parents' house. The college student wants to pick the right career and looks forward to meeting the person they will marry. The young married couple looks forward to having kids and owning their own home. The middle-aged married couple looks forward to when the kids are grown and out of the house. The older-aged married couple is looking forward to grandkids and retirement! (I apologize to the women reading this who are not married and may feel like they are stuck waiting to get married. I know your list will be different.) As Christians, we should find our contentment in Christ, *not* in attaining the next step in life! Driving a car, going to college, finding someone to marry, buying a house, having kids, and so on will not fill us or give us contentment, only God can do that.

What are other things people might look forward to or try to find their contentment in?

Do you have an area in your own life where you long for contentment? If so, write about it below.

According to Phil. 4:12, name the different ways that Paul had lived.

Paul had lived in *humble means* when he was hungry and suffering. He had also lived in prosperity when he had abundance and was filled and had all of his needs met. In both situations, he found the secret to contentment! I just want to stop and say that I just *love* that Paul calls this a secret! So, many people really do see contentment as a secret! They see it as a myth that isn't true. They think that there is no way they can be content in their everyday life. Paul (inspired by God) is about to reveal the secret!

Do you believe that God wants you to be content?

Write down Phil. 4:13 (the secret to being content).

Oh, Philippians 4:13. That special verse that almost every Christian, at some time in their life, has had as a favorite verse (other than John 3:16), but do we really understand this verse? Circle the first word. I think that many people read this Bible verse as a magic verse that means that they can do whatever they want to do, and then say "but it is okay because, 'I can do all things (and then they begin to fade out) through Christ who strengthens me.'" They do not put the focus on Christ who is the one giving the strength. They put the focus on themselves—the ones receiving the strength.

Some Christians think they can apply this verse wherever they want to. They think it can be applied with something that is small like trying to open a jar of jelly or winning a sports game, but what happens when we still can't open that jar or our team loses? Please do not get mad at me here. I am not saying that God does not care about you when you are trying to open that jar of jelly or when you are playing in that sports game, but I do think Paul had a deeper meaning than us just being able to magically call on God's strength at any time. Remember, Paul said this is the secret to being content. Some scholars believe that this verse should only be applied with economic matters (being rich or poor), but I think that since Paul also says "in any and every circumstance I have learned the secret" that we can apply this verse to other areas as long as we are talking about being content.

Only God's strength can give us contentment and peace when we lose our jobs and we don't know if we will be able to buy food for our family. Only God's strength can give us contentment and joy when we move away from all of our friends and loved ones to serve Him somewhere else. Only God can give us contentment and peace when we lose a loved one. Likewise, when we buy a new house, we will realize that house will not give us peace and contentment like God does. When we have a beautiful new baby, we will realize that our baby will never bring us true joy and contentment like God does. When we get a great new job making more money, we will realize that this new job will not bring us peace and contentment like God does. I believe this is the meaning behind Philippians 4:13. This is the secret to being content.

How can you apply this meaning of Philippians 4:13 to the area of your life where you long for contentment?

How do you feel when you read Phil. 4:13 in this new way? How do you think understanding Phil. 4:13 this way will help you in the future?

I hope that everyone reading this today will be able to find true contentment from Christ and not from anything else!

Week Six, Day Four: Closing Thoughts

Please begin today with prayer.

On the space below, write out your Bible verse for this week. Then, spend at least five minutes analyzing the scripture. Refer to day one so you can remember what you need to be looking for.

_____
_____
_____
_____
_____
_____
_____
_____
_____
_____
_____
_____
_____
_____
_____
_____

I must admit that I am sad that we are almost done with our study on the book of Philippians, but Paul keeps teaching to the very end of his letter, so don't think that there still isn't something we can learn from Paul's closing thoughts.

Read Phil. 4:15–16.

True or False: After Paul left Philippi, the church in Philippians was the only church to ever help him spread the Gospel.

Paul was very happy that the Church of Philippi helped support him and his ministry. From the beginning, the church members in Philippi helped Paul. Right after Paul left Philippi, he went to Thessalonica and the Church of Philippi sent him help right away.

The end of Philippians 4:15, Paul says, "No church shared with me in the matter of giving and receiving, but you alone." Let us look at the phrase *giving and receiving*.

What did the Philippians receive when Paul went to Philippi?

Paul shared the Gospel with them, and they then started sharing the Gospel and helping make sure Paul could continue *giving* the message of the Gospel to other people. They were so happy about receiving the gift of eternal life that they wanted to help other people get that same gift. Remember when we studied Paul's conversion in week one. He was immediately healed, and then he immediately started telling others about Jesus. You would think that more churches would have reacted the way that the Church of Philippi did. Why did they not? I don't doubt that they were very happy and excited about receiving enteral life, but maybe some of them saw it as just a way to get to heaven and not something that should change their lives, or maybe they were not willing to sacrificially give to help other ministries outside of their church. Go back to week four, day two and look at what we talked about with the passage Matthew 6:22–23. Maybe these churches did not have their eyes focused on heaven. Maybe they thought they were living in the light, but, really, they were not. I do not know why the Church of Philippi was the only church to give, but I do know that I want to be a member of a church like the one in Philippi.

Read Phil. 4:17–18.

What did Paul not seek?

Paul did not reach out to these Christians for their help, they offered on their own, and Paul told them that he sought the *profit which increases to your account.* Paul was happy that they would be rewarded by God for their gift.

What did Paul say that he had received?

Paul told them that they had given over and beyond in supporting him. Not only was Paul well supplied for his ministry at this point, but it would last him for a while.

What did Paul call their gift?

Paul is using language that was used in the Old Testament sacrificial system. Once again, Paul is saying to them that their sacrificial giving was very pleasing to God.

Since we have started this Bible study, we have talked a lot about giving more to help other ministries and making sure we are storing up treasures in heaven. Have you actually started sacrificing any earthly pleasures to help spread the Gospel? Why or why not?

Write down Phil. 4:19, and then circle the first word.

This is another one of those verses that Christians can easily take out of context. Christians might think that this is another magic verse that promises that God is going to take care of all of their needs. Yes, God does take care of Christians needs, but this verse has a deeper meaning. We need to connect this verse with Phil. 4:18. Which means that Paul is saying that because they were willing to sacrificially give to Paul's ministry, God was, in turn, going to provide for their needs.

Whose riches are supplied? (Verse 19)

If you realized that when you sacrificially give to help different ministries that God will in turn "supply all your needs according to His riches in glory in Christ Jesus," would you give more?

God is not always going to supply you with earthly riches. He will provide for your needs, but He will supply *His* riches!

Write down some examples of the riches that only God can provide.

Write down ways God has blessed you in your life with *His* riches.

I don't know about you, but I would rather have God's riches (things like joy and peace) more than earthly riches!

Read Phil. 4:20–22.

Who receives the glory?

Most likely, the thought of God blessing them brought God's majesty to mind, and the fact that, ultimately, we should all seek to bring glory to God. This is really the reason why we are here on this earth—to bring God glory. Everything in our lives should be about bringing glory to God.

Who does Paul want them to greet?

Paul wanted his greeting and his teachings to continue to other Christians around them, not just the Church of Philippi.

Who does Paul say greets them?

Paul includes greetings from the people who work and care for him in prison, all of the other Christians in Rome that Paul had contact with, and people who worked for the Roman government. Just like in the beginning of this letter, Paul was not going to leave anyone out. Some of these people might one day meet the Church of Philippi if Paul sent them with a message. Some of them might have already carried a message to them and the people who worked in the Roman government might visit them when they go visit Philippi.

Write down Phil. 4:23.

Paul ended his letter to the Philippians the same way he began it—by talking about grace. Paul started off praying grace and peace over the church, and now he ends by praying "the grace of the Lord Jesus Christ be with your spirit." It is through the Holy Spirit that we see God's grace in our lives. Our lives are full of God's grace; we just need to slow down enough to see His grace.

How has God shown you His grace in your everyday life?

I have noticed that there are many songs that talk about God's grace. I understand why it is such a popular song theme. I love driving down the road and hearing a song come on the radio about God's grace. It is a time when I am reminded that no matter what I am doing my life should revolve around God. Do you have a favorite song that talks about God's grace? If so, write the song below (you can even put a few lyrics down if you want to). I pray that from now on when you hear this song you will be remember that it is through God's grace that we are freed from our sins.

Paul followed Jesus all the way to his death. It is believed that he did get out of jail and was able to travel for some time. When Nero was in power, he sent people to look for Paul. They found Paul teaching others, and they asked Paul to pray for them. Paul prayed for them and told them that they could be baptized. I believe that Paul said this because either these people tried to make Paul think that they wanted to be Christians or Paul wanted to share with them how to become Christians. As soon as Paul said this, they took him away and he was beheaded. In the end, not only did Paul get to go to heaven to be with Jesus, but he had the privilege of suffering a death by persecution for His Lord! I pray that all of us will follow God with all of our hearts, all of our souls, and all of our strength all the way to our death, just like Paul did! Paul was a slave to Christ. He was persecuted. But because he was a slave of Christ's, he was freed from his bondage of sins and ultimately got to go live in heaven with his Savior and Lord.

Week Six, Day Five:
Week in Review

Today, I want you to begin with prayer (like all of the rest of the days). Pray that God will open your heart, speak to you, help you understand this scripture, show you how to apply these truths, and give you the power to apply His Word to your life. Make sure you pray for the requests that your group shared.

On the space below, write out your Bible verse for this week. Then, spend at least five minutes analyzing the scripture.

_____
_____
_____
_____
_____
_____
_____
_____
_____
_____
_____
_____
_____

I want for you to end this Bible study by sitting down and reading the whole book of Philippians. If you can, try to say it aloud while you read it. If you can't read it out loud, then listen to it on an audio Bible app while you read it at the same time. Soak in God's Word. Pray that God will open your heart. Pray He will speak to you. Pray God will help you understand this letter to the Church of Philippi. Pray that God will show you how to apply these truths. Pray God will give you the power to apply these truths.

Then without looking back on your notes, try to summarize what you learned from this book of the Bible. What did you learn about God's character from this book of the Bible? Did God specifically tell you to do something this week? Write your review and answers down. After you do this, go back and flip through the week and make any extra notes of things you forgot but you want to make sure you don't forget next time you read these passages.

_____

_____

_____

_____

_____

_____

_____

_____

_____

_____

_____

_____

_____

_____

Small Group Questions

1. Refer to your review day and take turns sharing with your group your summary of what happened in the scriptures you read this week.

2. What did God specifically teach you this week? Did God tell you to do something specific this week? Did you learn something new about God's character? If you need to, refer to the review day and take turns sharing with the group.

3. Share with each other areas that you are struggling with that you need prayer. Do not be scared to open up and share. God wants us to lift each other up in prayer. Ask for prayer that God will help you with anything He has told you to do. Write down everyone's prayer requests, and commit to praying for your friends during the week when you do this study. End your time together by praying specifically for each request.

_____

_____

_____

_____

_____

_____

_____

_____

_____

_____

_____

_____

_____

_____

Dear Friend,

I am a little sad to be done with writing the last day of this Bible study. I have learned so much from this book of the Bible, and God has shown me so much more than I ever imagined. I feel that as we end this Bible study that I should admit something to you. I started this Bible study because I have always been encouraged by this book of the Bible. Recently, God has told my husband and I that it is time to leave our current church. So, we are leaving, even if we do not know where God wants us to go next. We have looked. We have looked a lot! God has yet to show us where He wants us to go next. I am sad. Most of all, I do not want to leave my youth girls and the women in my Bible study group. This past year, I remember leaving Bible study and crying all the way home because I was so sad that God wants us to leave. These women are my friends and I love them. Sometimes at night when my husband goes to sleep, I cry when I think about the fact that I am going to miss three of my youth girls' senior years. I am not going to be here with them as they make the final decisions on which college to go to and what to major in. I am not going to be here when they are stressed over having enough money to get into college or when they decide how they are going to decorate their dorm rooms. I will miss them, and this breaks my heart. And now (like Paul), I am actually crying while I write this.

But even with all of this sadness, I have found peace. I know that God is going to complete what He started with these youth girls and the women in the Bible study group. I have peace that even if we do not know where we are going that God will take care of us. Now after doing this study, I know that I will be a better church member at my next church. I will seek unity. I will not be arrogant. This study has changed my life. I thank you for going on the journey with me.

As we end our journey together, I pray that God has spoken to you through this study. I pray that you have been encouraged. I pray that you have found unity in an area where you needed unity. I pray that you have found peace with God. I pray that you are striving to live your life in obedience to God, not out of ritual but because you love Him and realize all He has done for you. I pray that you will reach out to the people around you and share the love of Christ with others. I pray that you will give sacrificially to ministries and missionaries. I pray that you have found contentment in God. I pray that you will look forward to the sanctification process where you are freed from the bondage of more and more sin. I pray that when you fail (and we all do), that you will remember that God's grace covers you and will keep you going. I pray that you will rejoice in the Lord, and keep your eyes and heart focused on Him every day.

Your friend,

AJ Paris

Week One

1. Chan, Francis. *Multiply*. Colorado Springs, CO: David C. Cook, 2012. 93–95.
2. Ibid., 96–103.
3. Ibid., 115 and 121.
4. Ibid., 112–114.
5. Warren, Kay. *Choose Joy*. Grand Rapids: Revell, 2012. 101.
6. Chan. 98–99.
7. Duvell, J. Scott and J. Daniel Hays. *Grasping God's Word*. Grand Rapids: Zondervan, 2001. 39.
8. Moore, Ralph. *Making Disciples*. Ventura, CA: Regal, 2012. 151.
9. Smith, Angie. *Seamless Bible Study*. Nashville: LifeWay, 2017. 137.
10. Quarles, Charles L. "Paul." *Holman Illustrated Bible Dictionary*. Nashville: Holman Bible Publishers, 2003. 1255–1256.
11. Melick Jr., Richard R. *The New American Commentary: Philippians, Colossians and Philemon*. Nashville: Broadman Press, 1991. 26–28.
12. Polhill, John B. *The New American Commentary: Acts*. Nashville: Broadman Press, 1992. 345–349.
13. Ibid., 354.
14. Ibid., 357.

Week Two

1. Melick. 47–51.
2. Kent Jr., Homer A. *The Expositor's Bible Commentary: Philippians*. Grand Rapids: Zondervan, 1978. 103–104.

3. Ibid., 105–108.
4. Moore. 154.
5. Melick. 66.
6. Goodrick, Edward W., John R. Kohlenberger III, James A. Swanson. *Zondervan NIV Exhaustive Concordance, 2nd Ed.* Grand Rapids: Zondervan, 1990. 1463.
7. Kent. 109–112.
8. Ibid., 113–117.
9. Concordance. 5401.
10. Platt, David. *Follow Me.* Tyndale Publishing, 2013. 105–106.

Week Three

1. Melick. 88–92.
2. Polhill. 347.
3. Melick. 92–95.
4. Dictionary.com
5. Rainer, Thom. *I am a Church Member.* Nashville: B & H Publishing Group, 2013.
6. Melick. 96–109.
7. Ibid., 110.
8. Platt. 17–29.

Week Four

1. Melick. 110–115.
2. Blomberg, Craig L. *The New American Commentary: Matthew.* Nashville: Broadman Press, 1992. 122–127.
3. Melick. 116–122.

4. Moore. 100–107.
5. Melick. 126–128.
6. Ibid., 129–135.

Week Five

1. Melick. 129–135.
2. Ibid.,129–135.
3. Ibid., 135–141.
4. Kent. 141–143.
5. Grudem, Wayne. *Systematic Theology*. Grand Rapids: Zondervan Publishing House, 1994. 723–724.
6. Ibid., 746–753.
7. Melick. 141–144.
8. Kent. 149–150.
9. Melick. 148–149.

Week Six

1. Warren. 31.
2. Kent. 151.
3. Ibid., 151–153.
4. Melick. 149–151.
5. Warren. 72.
6. Melick. 152–156.
7. Ibid., 156–159.
8. Foxe, John. *Foxe's Book of Martyrs*. Uhrichsville, OH: Barbour Publishing, 2005. 17.

About the Author

AJ Paris spent the past ten years as a stay-at-home mother to her two wonderful children (Juliette and James), and was also heavily involved in helping her husband (Jason) in his ministry. Recently, her family has moved back to her hometown and she now teaches public school students the Bible through a program called Release Time. AJ has a passion for teaching the Bible, and helping other women apply its truths to their daily lives. She graduated from North Greenville University with a BA in Christian Studies.

CPSIA information can be obtained
at www.ICGtesting.com
Printed in the USA
LVHW04s0808300718
585356LV00003BA/253/P